Langford Cecil

Fenacre Grange

Vol. II

Langford Cecil

Fenacre Grange
Vol. II

ISBN/EAN: 9783337041120

Printed in Europe, USA, Canada, Australia, Japan

Cover: Foto ©ninafisch / pixelio.de

More available books at **www.hansebooks.com**

FENACRE GRANGE.

A Novel.

BY

LANGFORD CECIL.

IN THREE VOLUMES.
VOL. II.

LONDON:
TINSLEY BROTHERS, 18, CATHERINE STREET, STRAND.
1870.

[*All rights of Translation and Reproduction are reserved.*]

CONTENTS

OF

THE SECOND VOLUME.

CHAP.		PAGE
I.	BEHIND THE SCENES	1
II.	IN A SPONGING-HOUSE	34
III.	ROTTEN ROW	61
IV.	LADY GEORGE'S THEATRICALS	89
V.	MR. SMALL'S PRYINGS	114
VI.	ON BOULOGNE PIER	141
VII.	MADELEINE REFUSES A DUKE'S ELDEST SON	169
VIII.	SIR JOHN IN PARIS	195
IX.	MADELEINE MAKES A CONQUEST	218
X.	SISTER MONICA	242
XI.	MAJOR MANDARIN GETS CHECKMATED	264

FENACRE GRANGE.

CHAPTER I.

BEHIND THE SCENES.

"Half the world do not know how the other half live."
OLD PROVERB.

E began the last chapter by saying that all before the curtain were pious, moral, and well-conducted, and that all behind the scenes were universally accredited with the contrary attributes; we have seen those who think they are so eminently endowed with "all the virtues." We will now take a glimpse at those whom they despise,

and yet at the same time condescend to be amused by them; in the meantime ascribing to them "all the vices" of which, of course, they themselves are as guiltless as a bran-new baby.

Lady George and her party had to wait some time before the *employés* at "Her Highness's" began to leave the theatre; it took them some little time to resume their ordinary habiliments.

"I wish they'd look sharp and come out," said Lady George. "I'm tired of waiting here."

Lady Fenacre was scanning each face anxiously as the door opened and shut again: she had seen a countenance only too well known to her, yet she dared not hope it was him. He was drowned, and the grave could not have given up its dead! Yet she hoped and suffered silently.

A man in a long, grey great-coat, was

skulking about outside the stage-door; he passed and repassed Lady George's brougham, till at last she remarked it.

"I wonder what that fellow is loafing about for?" said her ladyship. "I suppose he's waiting to see one of the *coryphées*."

Lady Fenacre looked out of the window as the man passed quite close to the carriage; she caught sight of his face, and recognised him instantly: the man in the great-coat was Mr. Small, of the private inquiry office, near the Strand.

Mr. Small, attired in an irreproachable suit of sables and the regulation white tie, had witnessed the performance of "Faust" from the stalls. He had scanned the soldiers with his powerful *lorgnettes*, and it had struck him that the second front rank man was very like a photograph he had at that moment in his waistcoat-pocket.

He took out the photograph and looked

at it; then he looked on to the stage. "If it's not him, I'm a fool—that's all!" he said to himself, as he replaced the portrait. "I shall go round and watch those fellows as they come out," he continued.

This was the reason why Mr. Small was passing up and down the pavement in front of Lady George Fitzreine's brougham.

The chorus-singers began to follow closely upon one another: they were mostly of the description of men who are aptly termed "shabby-genteel!"— that is, they were broken-down individuals who had seen better days; some of them scions of good families who had been turned adrift by their relatives on account of their strong *penchant* "to go to the dogs!" they were not fit for hard manual labour, nor close desk-work. The desultory work of going on to the stage for an hour or two every night suited them better than regular employment, even if they could have it. Besides, people must live, and it is better to earn an honest living by singing an infinity of "tral lal la," for the amusement of her Majesty's lieges, than to write whining begging letters in the newspapers, beseeching the help of "kind Christian friends!" It is a much more honest and honourable thing to do to support oneself instead of "sponging" on the benevolence of the charitable; even by the wicked device of singing "tral lal la" in a brass hat on a public stage!

Mr. Small went up the stone steps leading to the stage-door and went in. The doorkeeper knew him very well, and asked no questions as he passed; the "property-men" who were rolling-up the scenes were not a bit surprised when he walked on to the stage; they all knew him by sight—in fact, he was a man who walked in and out where he pleased. If he had gone into a Freemasons' lodge during the mysterious initiation, the "brethren" wouldn't have kicked him out: he was a privileged man, and could go *anywhere!*

"Have you anybody new in the chorus to-night?" asked Mr. Small of the stage-manager.

"One young fellow," replied Doldrum. "I fancy he's some swell, who hasn't 'hit it' with his friends. We often have them in the chorus. Lord Mountchessington's son sung every night in the 'Huguenots' last season!"

"When he got into that scrape at Pluto's," said Mr. Small; "I remember."

"Yes, that's when it was," said Doldrum. "We rather like having those young swells in the chorus; they sing better than your common chaps," he continued.

"I should like to stand somewhere where I could see them all go out without being seen," said Mr. Small.

"All right: stand here," said Doldrum; "you will see them all pass."

Then he concealed Mr. Small behind a "rock" (it was only a canvas one), and took leave of him, wishing he might find his friend.

Mr. Small had hardly hid himself when the chorus came trooping out. Some were laughing and talking loudly, others were walking in silence and not opening their lips to any one.

"He'll be one of the silent ones," said Mr. Small to himself.

The very last man in the procession was an aristocratic-looking man of about seven-and-twenty, looking very pale, haggard, and dejected. He walked after the others as if he were in a dream. Their mirth and jollity seemed to jar and grate upon his nerves.

"Has it come to this?" he murmured to

himself. "Oh, Nelly! I am glad you think me dead; it is better than your knowing how wretched I am!"

The passage was narrow, so the foremost of the party blocked up the exit into the street; this caused a complete stoppage to those in the rear. The man at the tail of the procession stopped just opposite to the "rock" behind which Mr. Small had concealed himself; there was a little hole in the canvas which Mr. Small could see through.

"It *is* him," said the detective, pulling out the photograph, "and I'll go and tell her ladyship I've run him to earth, the very first thing to-morrow morning."

Then the procession passed on; the foremost had gained the street.

When the men had passed, Mr. Small came out from his hiding place, and walked about the mazes of cordage, lifts, trap-doors, and windlasses, which constitute the realm "behind the scenes." The stage is not flat, as it appears from view "before the curtain," but shelves gradually down from the back of the house to the footlights. Mr. Small walked about, and whilst doing so, hazarded conjectures as to what Lady Fenacre would give him for his intelligence. "She ought to pay handsome," he said to himself. "No one but myself could have found him out."

When the object of Mr. Small's espionage got to the door, he stood for a moment under the flaring gas-lamp.

Lady Fenacre was looking, and recognised him. She trembled so violently and was so agitated that she could not speak. He only stood for a moment, and he was lost again in that labyrinth of brick and mortar called London.

Lady George was getting impatient.

"All the men have come out; where are the

women? I suppose they keep them separate, like they do at Whitey Brown's!" she said.

"Mamselle Squalini's carriage!" shouts one of the linkmen, and out comes the *prima donna*, who has just been electrifying the town with her wonderful powers of song.

"Here they come," said Lady George. "What a time they have been dressing again, to be sure; longer than it could have taken them to take off their 'properties,' I expect."

Two or three of the very naughty ones had broughams, and drove home to their villas in St. John's Wood; those who were poor, but virtuous, had to walk home in the rain. It is the retribution of this world.

A pale, pretty-looking woman, dressed in deep mourning, came out, and Lady George instantly recognised her. "Go and tell that woman in black I want to speak to her, there's a good fellow," said Lady George to Fitzcharles.

Fitzcharles jumped out of the brougham, and ran up the street.

"Lady George Fitzreine wants to speak to you," said Fitzcharles, when he overtook her.

The woman hurried on without turning her head: she was used to being spoken to rudely as she went home to her children, and she thought it was only some passing freak of one of the "Champagne Charlie" species: so she hurried on.

"Will you stop, please?" said Fitzcharles. "Lady George Fitzreine asked me to tell you she wanted to see you."

Mrs. Ewart (for it was she) stopped, and turned round. When she caught sight of Fitzcharles' face it inspired her with confidence. "A boy like that is too fresh from the influence of his mother and sisters to insult a woman," she thought to herself; so she stopped and let him catch her up.

Just then a brougham dashed up to the pavement, and Lady George jumped out, almost before the servant could get the door opened.

"You *must* let me drive you home," said Lady George. "Why did not you tell me you were reduced to this? I've got enough for myself, and some to spare for you."

"Because I would rather *earn* my bread than be beholden for it to my dearest friends," said Mrs. Ewart.

"You might have asked me, surely," said Lady George.

"No; I would rather do *anything* than beg," replied Mrs. Ewart—"even of you."

The fact was, that when Lady George had first been to see Mrs. Ewart, she had given her all she had in her purse, about fifteen pounds, and had then gone away and forgotten all about her till she saw her on the stage at "Her Highness's." Like most warm-hearted, impulsive people, Lady George did not think much about any one whom she was not continually meeting. Her time was so occupied with the business of pleasure that she had no time to think about anyone who was not in her "set."

Mrs. Ewart began to cough. It was a dry, hacking cough, that shook her whole frame.

"You ought not to be out on a wet night like this," said Lady George.

"I can't help it," said Mrs. Ewart. "If I was to miss one night, I should lose my engagement, and then my children would starve again. I would rather anything than they should suffer."

Then she coughed again.

"You will let me drive you home!" said Lady George.

"No, thank you," she replied. "The people in the court would begin to talk if I came from the theatre in a carriage. Thank you, I'd rather not."

"*Do* let me do something for you!" said Lady George. "I can't bear to see you looking so ill, and having such a fearful cough."

"The stage is very draughty," said Mrs. Ewart. "I caught cold the first night, and it's got worse ever since. But I can't give it up."

"Maud," said Lady George, "have you ever asked your brother-in-law, Sir John Fenacre, to help you?"

Mrs. Ewart's thin, pale cheeks flushed crimson, but she did not answer.

"What did he say?" said Lady George.

"He said, No!" replied Mrs. Ewart, hoarsely. "I would never have asked him if it had not been for the children's sake. And I would rather die working for them than ever ask him again!"

"I think he's not disinclined to do something for you," said Lady George. "He spoke of it to me."

Mrs. Ewart started, and stared with astonishment.

"Sir John do anything for me!" she exclaimed. "Why, he nearly drove me out of the house. And oh! he spoke so cruelly of poor Claude."

"He is willing to give you four pounds a week," said Lady George; "and it's to come through me."

"Then he has relented; and, for poor Minnie's sake, will help my fatherless children!" said Mrs. Ewart. "I did not think he could be so cruel for long. I knew a father's heart must have some pity in it for others. He could not be so cruel!"

"Oh, he's got reasons of his own," said Lady George; "so don't ascribe it to any kind, natural feeling on his part! He only makes one condition—that you give up the stage."

"That will not stand in his way," said Mrs. Ewart. "I've been longing to do it. Besides, it makes my cough so bad, being out at night."

Four pounds a week seemed a perfect fortune to her. She only earned a guinea at "Her Highness's," and most of her time was occupied by rehearsals.

"*Do* thank Sir John for me," said Mrs. Ewart. "It's *so* good of him."

"You needn't thank him," said Lady George; "he has his own reasons for doing it. But you mustn't stand out in the rain any longer, you're wet through already. I shall come to-morrow and bring the money. Good night!"

Mrs. Ewart could not answer, for a violent fit of coughing came on, and she was obliged to lean against the lamp-post for support. "This is the last night I shall have to walk home alone through these miserable streets," she said to herself. "Thank God for it!" Then she hurried on.

The pavements were quite deserted, save by a few of the wretched, painted phantoms that flaunt about the streets of great cities after dark. They raised a mocking laugh as she fled past them, "Are you not one of us?" they cried after her; then laughed again dismally.

When Mrs. Ewart got back to the garret she called her "home," she found a fire burning brightly and a kettle singing on the hob. It was the kind forethought of the landlady. Lazarus has more pity for his fellows in distress than Dives: the latter will say, "Be ye clothed," and not lift his little finger to bring it to pass; the former will make you welcome to half his scanty store.

Mrs. Ewart sat down by the fire in her wet clothes, and began to warm herself; the water on them began to steam like a vapour bath: the steam made her cough.

"You mustn't go no more to sing," said the old woman who came in with a hot cup of tea. "You mustn't indeed, dear."

"I am not going any more," she replied. "I've got a fortune given me. I'm going to have four pounds a week!" Then she laughed hysterically.

"Don't take it, dear," said the old woman. "Better to starve, and keep honest. I'll do what I can to help you. Please don't take his money," she continued, entreatingly.

"Why not?" said Mrs. Ewart. "Why not? When my children will be clothed and fed?"

"Because the wages of sin is death," said the old woman, solemnly.

"What do you mean?" said Mrs. Ewart, staring with astonishment. "I don't understand what you mean."

"I mean, dear, that you are young and pretty; and poverty has such awful temptations, that you should be careful how you tamper with gold. It's ruined more souls than any single thing on earth!"

"Leave the room!" cried Mrs. Ewart, starting to her feet. "How dare you insult me like this? Leave the room!" She then sat down by the fire, and buried her face in her hands, and moaned. She was moaning because she was in pain, and sobbing with indignation.

"Oh, do forgive me, dear," said the old woman. "I didn't mean to offend you. I only spoke for the best. For pity's sake, forgive me. One of my own girls is lost to me, and I felt a mother's craving to save you. For pity's sake, forgive me!"

she continued, throwing herself on her knees.

"I forgive you," said Mrs. Ewart. "I forgot what I was when I was indignant with you. It was very natural you should think as you did. I ought to have told you that the money was coming to me, from a brother-in—— I mean a member of my family."

"Do take off your wet things," said the old woman. Then she helped her to undress.

Mrs. Ewart walked up to the cribs where the children were lying asleep. They were pretty children, with golden hair, but their cheeks looked rather pinched. "I shall be able to take them into the country now," said the mother to herself, as she bent over them, and kissed them. As she kissed them they smiled. "They are dreaming of the angels," she said to herself. Then she went to bed.

She was not, however, able to sleep. She

coughed incessantly. The old woman, who slept in the next room, heard her, and got up and came to her.

"Drink this, dear," she said, holding a glass of water to her lips; "it will do you good."

"I have got such a pain here," said Mrs. Ewart, pointing to her chest. "It kills me every time I cough."

"Try and go to sleep," said the old woman.

"I can't," said Mrs. Ewart. "When I shut my eyes I see stars and rays of gold light."

"I'll make up the fire and sit with you," said the landlady; "it will be more comfortable for you."

The poor woman had to work hard all day, yet she willingly and cheerfully gave up her night's rest for a stranger in distress. I doubt whether Dives would have done so; he would have gone away saying, "I hope you will have a good night," and ensconced himself in the blankets, and thought nothing more about it.

Mrs. Ewart coughed at intervals during the night. Between the fits she lay with her eyes wide open, in a kind of trance.

It was summer, and the grey light of morning began to break over the housetops.

"Pull up the blind, please," said Mrs. Ewart. "I want to see the sky."

The old woman complied with her request, and the room gradually became filled with grey light.

"It reminds me of mornings long ago," she continued, "when I was happy at home, without a thought or care for the future. I don't know why, but something of the same feeling seems to be stealing over me now."

The rays of the sun were gilding the

weathercocks on the church-steeples, and it was soon broad daylight.

The light woke the children, and they sat up in their beds and began to play. Their mother watched them silently for some time; at length the tears began to trickle down her cheek: she was thinking what would become of them if she was to die.

"I don't feel as if I should live long," she said. "I don't know how to describe the feeling, but I have it."

"Don't talk like that, dear," said the old woman. "I can't abear to hear you. You'll soon get well again, when you get a nice little cottage in the country, amongst woods and green fields."

Mrs. Ewart tried to answer her, but her cough was getting worse, and prevented her from speaking.

The morning wore on, and about eleven

o'clock a tap was heard at the door, and Lady George came in.

"Good morning, Maud," she said, and went up to the bed and kissed her.

Mrs. Ewart smiled faintly, her breath was getting so laboured she could not speak.

"I have brought you the money," said Lady George.

Mrs. Ewart smiled again, and pointed to the children, who were playing on the floor.

Lady George knew by instinct what she meant, though she could not speak.

Just then she heard the landlady outside, so she opened the door to speak to her. The old woman made a sign for her to come into her room.

"I don't think the poor thing is long for here," she said; "her cough is awful, and she came in wet through last night, and it's gone to her chest."

"Have you sent for a doctor?" said Lady George.

"No; it's no use. He wouldn't come here if I did," said the landlady. "They never get paid here, so they leave the poor to die as they can."

"I will see what I can do to get one," said Lady George. "I'll go at once."

Then she went down stairs, and got in her brougham, and drove to Sir Alfred Kempe's.

Sir Alfred Kempe was the fashionable doctor, so his waiting-room was crammed.

"Give this card to Sir Alfred," said Lady George to the servant, as he opened the door.

On her card she had written, "I want to see you immediately."

The servant showed her into the waiting-room; in another moment he opened the door and said, "Will Lady George Fitzreine walk this way, please?"

The other patients looked savage : they had been waiting for hours, and she had only been in a minute.

"If she'd only known what a state my liver is in, she'd have let me go first," said Colonel Chutnee, of the Bengal Tigers.

"Good morning, Lady George," said Sir Alfred. "What can I do for you this morning ?"

"Oh, I want you to come with me, this minute, to see a poor woman."

"Impossible !" said Sir Alfred, decidedly. "Perfectly impossible !"

"Oh ! but you *must !*" said Lady George. " It's a case of life and death !"

"I have got a room full of patients to see," said Sir Alfred. " They'll be furious."

" Let 'em !" said Lady George; " they're only a lot of pigs who have gorged themselves to such an extent during the season, that they've got dyspepsia at the end of it."

Sir Alfred laughed. He knew this was perfectly true. "If they see me going out of the front door they'll all bolt," he said.

"Come out at the back, then," said Lady George, taking hold of his hand, and looking up into his face. "Please do!"

Sir Alfred was mortal. It's a hard matter to say "No" to a pretty woman, when she very much wants you to say "Yes," so he said, " Very well, I'll come; but you mustn't keep me."

Then he rang the bell.

"Tell Lady George Fitzreine's coachman to drive round to the mews, and wait at the stable-door," he said to the servant. Then he got his coat and hat. "If they ask for me, say I have an important consultation in *here*. It would never do for the B. P. to think I am going to take the trouble to go and see *them*—they must come to me."

Then the Doctor and Lady George went out over the leads, through the stable, and got into her brougham in the mews.

"It's like an elopement," said Sir Alfred. "Wont the British Lion growl in my waiting-room!"

In the half-hour Lady George had been absent, she found a great change in Mrs. Ewart: she was looking so pale and white.

Sir Alfred went up to the bed, and pulled out his stethoscope, and applied it to her chest. He shook his head, and whispered to Lady George, "She can't last many hours: it's inflammation of the lungs. I can do nothing: it's too late."

Lady George slipped his fee into his hand, and said, "You'd better take my carriage back, and then tell the man to go home: I shall stay here till the end." Then she shook hands with the Doctor, and he left.

"Drive to the stable-door again," he said to the servant as he got in, and before many minutes he was back in his room in Harley Street.

"You may show Colonel Chutnee in," he said to the servant. "Sorry that an important consultation has kept me so long," he said to the gallant Colonel on his entry.

"Sorry!" said the Colonel; "you *ought* to be sorry, sir! Why was that woman let in first? If she had only known the state my liver's in, she wouldn't have had the heart to have done it, sir! I am *sure* she wouldn't!"

When the Doctor left, Lady George took a chair by Mrs. Ewart's bedside, and held her hand.

The dying woman was murmuring something in a low voice. Lady George bent down her head to try and catch what she said. She was evidently wandering, for she was talking of her husband as if he were present, and she was entreating him not to go to some place the name of which Lady George could not make out.

At length she started up in the bed and gazed wildly round the room. "Where am I?" she cried; then lay down again, apparently exhausted.

It is often the case that a short time before death a rally takes place; this rally has often deceived fond patient watchers by a sick-bed. It is but the gathering of all the powers of nature for the final struggle.

Mrs. Ewart seemed to gain strength. After a few moments, she was able to speak.

"Where are the children?" she said. "I want them."

The old woman had taken them down into her room, so as to keep the room quiet.

Lady George went and fetched them, and put them on their mother's bed.

"Now I am happy," she said, and smiled. A cloud, however, came over her face, and she began to feel about anxiously.

"Where's Claude?" she said, at length. "Oh, I remember; he was lost that fearful night. Lost! lost! lost!"

She said this with a kind of despairing hollowness.

"Christ came to seek the lost," said Lady George, gently. "And he will be found again in the infinite love and compassion of God."

"Talk to me like that," said the dying woman. "It's as good as seeing a clergyman."

"We want no priest as a mediator between us and God. We have one high priest and mediator, our Lord and Saviour Jesus Christ," said Lady George.

"I am afraid I've been a great sinner, and haven't thought of these things as I ought," said Mrs. Ewart.

"God is love," said Lady George, "and love covereth all sins."

"If I could live my life over again, I would act very differently," said Mrs. Ewart.

"So the best of us say when we come to die. All that is required of us is penitence and faith. The rest was done for us on Calvary," said Lady George. "If you believe on the Lord Jesus Christ, you are saved."

"I believe with my whole heart," said Mrs. Ewart, and as she said these words she fell back dead. She had burst a blood-vessel.

The old woman came in, and seeing the sheets deluged with blood, she screamed and burst into tears. "Oh! those poor children!" she cried. "What will become of them?"

"I will see to that," said Lady George, who was arranging the tumbled bed-clothes. "Here's some money for them to go on with." Then she placed in the landlady's hand the four pounds she had received that morning from Sir John Fenacre.

"Thank you, my lady," said the old woman.

Lady George walked home very slowly and sadly. "What *is* this world, that one loves it so!" she thought.

"Worldlings" have this thought when they are confronted with misery and death, just like other people, though Whitey Brown says they have not!

CHAPTER II.

IN A SPONGING-HOUSE.

"Stone walls do not a prison make,
Nor iron bars a cage."

LORD HENRY FITZREINE was sitting in the private parlour of a sheriff's officer, in Whitecross Street, gazing ruefully in the fire. He had been arrested that morning at the suit of Major Mandarin, his *ci-devant* bosom friend.

Queen was moralizing on the immutability of friendship, and the deceitfulness of mankind in general. He had the same feeling as the psalmist had, when he wrote, "For it was not an enemy," &c. It *is* mortifying to find the wolf under the sheep's clothing!

"By Jove!" said Queen to himself, "it's too bad! I was like a brother to him. I got him into the 'Tag,' and into society. He'd have been black-balled to a dead certainty if it hadn't been for me; and this is the thanks and gratitude I get for it. By Jove! it's *too* bad."

The door opened, and the subject of Queen's soliloquy came in.

He was dressed in a black frock-coat and a broad-brimmed hat. If you were to meet him in the street you would say, "What a respectable man!" We who are behind the scenes know to the contrary.

"Morning, old fellow!" said the Major. "Sorry to see you in this mess."

"It's all your doing," said Queen, fiercely.

"Don't excite yourself, my dear sir,"

said the Major. "Agitation is bad for the nervous system."

"—— the nervous system!" said Queen.

"Really we couldn't do without it," said the Major, blandly. "I have been to see Sir Alfred, and he says your brother's fits are all moonshine, and that the German baths will set him all right again; therefore, sir, you obtained money from me under false pretences—under false pretences, sir!" he continued, fiercely.

"They all say at home he can't live," said Queen. "You should have made these inquiries before you lent me this money."

"I *thought*," said the Major, significantly—"I *thought* I was dealing with a gentleman, but it seems I was vastly mistaken."

Queen looked into the fire and did not answer; his conscience smote him for having represented his brother worse than he was: besides, he had some feeling of fraternal affection, and he did not like to think he had been trafficking with his death.

"I'll let you out on one condition," said the Major. "And it's a very easy one, too."

"What is it?" said Queen, anxiously.

"A *post obit* on your father," replied the money-lender.

"No, I wont do it," said Queen, decisively.

"It wont make him die any sooner," said the Major.

"I know that, but I don't like to do it all the same. I shouldn't like a son of mine to do it to me," said Queen.

"There's no fear of that," said the Major, "because no one would accept his bill. You've got nothing yourself, and nothing to leave in consequence."

This was a home-thrust at poor Queen. He knew it was true, so he kept silence.

"I'll have the papers prepared this afternoon, and bring them this evening," said the Major. "You have only got to put 'Henry Fitzreine' at the bottom of them, and you are a free man to-night!"

Liberty is a tempting lure: it is an innate feeling in the heart. The cry once raised has bathed nations in seas of blood, animated men to the utmost pitch of heroism: and yet withal, how many crimes have been committed in her sacred name! Liberty is a kind of Juggernaut, before whose car men have laid down their lives in blind frenzy, without really knowing for *what* they perish; they perish for a phantom, an idea, a chimera!—they do not know what.

In a minor degree this feeling influenced Queen. His one idea was "liberty," and *any* scheme to attain it appeared perfectly legitimate in his eyes. He was not one of the immaculate "goody" tribe who *never* fall; he was merely a poor "worldling," so he tumbled, after a few demurs, into the crafty trap.

In plain English, he consented to sign the *post obit*.

It is considered very dreadful and unnatural to do a *post obit*, and perhaps it is; but I must confess I should not mind it being done to me,—that is, if I was told of it. I should not like it if I was not. If the heir to my vast estates were to say to me, "I've done a *post obit* on you," I should reply, "All right, you are welcome to 'do' as many as you please, and I hope I shall live for many years during which you will have to pay the interest on the capital you have borrowed. You are a great fool, because you wont enjoy the property when you *do* get it. But please yourself; you can't have it now and at a future time as well."

The real evil of *post obits* is the encouragement of extravagance and waste. As to the unnatural part of the story, I say the same to the theory as the sunbeam did to the rosebud—viz., " You be blowed." It's all moonshine and sentimental balderdash.

"I can't stick in this dull hole," said Queen, "so I'll do it. Though I must say I don't like it."

Here we see that the desire for liberty was inducing Queen to do what was contrary to his natural feelings and inclination. Verily, she is a potent goddess.

Major Mandarin took his leave, promising to bring the necessary documents in the evening. When he was gone, Queen thought, " Well, I've said I'll do it, so I must. I'll tell the governor some night after dinner. I wonder whether he'll mind it. Daresay he did it himself, if the truth was known."

This latter idea pleased and comforted Lord Henry. I have heard some say, when reproved by stern paterfamilias for their youthful follies and peccadilloes, "I daresay he used to do the same himself."

Very likely he did. In fact, there is no doubt of it; but it is his duty all the same to pitch into you. You will do the same when you are " prefects, fathers of families, game-preservers, and councillors of state."

Being a "Lord" of course Queen had a private room—and had to pay for it accordingly—thirty-five shillings a day was he charged for board and lodging. The former consisted of greasy mutton chops and fiery sherry; and the latter of a dingy parlour. But if people, by their imprudence and wasteful extravagance, find themselves in sponging-houses, they must put up with all discomforts and disagreeables they may find therein.

At two o'clock Queen had his luncheon. As he was a "Lord," the bailiff's daughter had gone upstairs and put on her best dress to bring it in to him herself. She had adorned her black hair with red velvet, and she wore a sky-blue silk dress. However, all this was lost upon Queen, who did not speak to her.

"Is there *anything* more you want?" she said at length, when she had fiddled the cruets about, and smoothed the cloth till she could not do so any longer.

"To be left alone," said Queen, curtly.

Miss Moses bounced out of the room and banged the door.

"That fellow in there's like a bear," she said to her mother. Then she went upstairs and took off her silk dress. "Catch me taking in his victuals again!" she said, as she folded it up and put it away in the drawer.

Miss Moses sometimes had great fun with the "birds" who filled her father's cage.

Meanwhile Queen sat and sipped the fiery sherry. The sherry made him feel sentimental. "By Jove!" he said, "I'm like the prisoner of Chillon, or Richard I. in the hands of the Duke of Austria. Oh! for a Blondel!" he sighed.

"A note for you, my lord," said a dirty maid-of-all-work, as she opened the door, and half put her head in.

Lord Henry got up and took it from her. Her thumb-mark was round and black on the envelope.

"Why don't you wash your hands?" he said.

"That fellow in there's like a bear!" said the handmaid, when she got back in the kitchen among her fellows. " I never seed such a one !"

When the servant was gone, Lord Henry tore the note open eagerly. It was from his brother, and ran thus:—

" Albany.

" Dear Henry,—I hear you are in a mess. Can I help you ? Let me know how much you want, and I'll pay it to your account at Dock's.
" Yours,
" Dagenham.

" June 31, 18 — ."

" He's a good fellow," said Queen, " and always ready to give one a help. And here have I been specking on his death. What a brute I am ! I don't like taking his money, after all I've said and done. 'Pon my word, I don't !"

Then Queen sat down, and meditated gloomily. He began to think of Richard I.

and Blondel. An idea flashed across him, and he got up and rang the bell.

Necessity is the mother of invention, and adversity sharpened the imaginative powers of Lord Henry. He had actually originated an idea—and that was a great and unusual feat for him—he thought himself a Fouché at once.

The dirty maid came in.

"Tell Miss Moses I should be so much obliged to her if she would give me a cup of coffee," said Queen; "also, that I should like to see her."

Miss Moses did not bear malice, so she flew upstairs and changed her dress again, and put the red velvet in her hair.

" He's coming round," she said to herself. " They are usually a bit rusty when they are first nabbed—which is but natural!"

Then she went down and took in his coffee.

"Wont you sit down?" said Queen; "I'm very lonely here all day by myself."

Miss Moses sat down at once: she did not require any pressing whatever.

"I wish I'd got Mandarin's head here," said Queen, as he made a lunge at the empty grate with the poker.

"Law! my lord!" said Miss Moses, "how vindictory you are!"

"I wish I had!" said Queen, again. "I'd give something to be out of this," he continued.

"I daresay you would," said Miss Moses; "but it ain't so easy."

"But is it possible?" said Queen.

"Nothing's impossible to a willing man," she replied.

"You're a nice-looking girl," said Queen, "and I am willing to kiss you." Then he did it.

"Go along! for shame!" said Miss Moses,

all the time feeling very much pleased and gratified.

"Come and sit on my knee," said Queen, dragging her towards him.

Miss Moses was nothing loth, nor was she particular, or what girls call "proper," so she went without any great resistance.

"If you'll help me to get out of this, I'll give you a necklace and bracelets—by Jove, I will!" said Queen.

"I daren't," said Miss Moses; "father would half kill me."

"He need never know it," said Queen.

"I can't do it," said Miss Moses, "though I should like the necklace and bracelets. I should like to cut out those horrid Smith girls next Sabbath," she continued.

"Nothing easier," said Queen. "You've only got to give me a wrinkle, and they are your own."

"One of those bars *is* rather loose," said

Miss Moses, looking towards the window; "and it ain't above a six-feet drop on to the leads."

"Hurrah!" said Queen. "I'll sell old Mandarin! What a rage he'll be in when he finds his bird flown! I shall want a screwdriver," said Queen.

"I'll bring you one," replied Miss Moses.

"You're a brick!" said Queen: "a regular brick—you are indeed!"

And I'm afraid he kissed her again, but am not quite sure, not being present. You should believe *nothing* you hear, and only *half* you see.

"What kind of a chap is he?" said Mrs. Moses to her daughter, when she came out of the parlour.

"Oh! he's a jolly h'affable kind of chap," she replied, "and very free with his money."

"Let him have his things a bit nice,

then," said Mrs. Moses. "You'd better see to it yourself."

At six o'clock Miss Moses took in the dinner. In the potato-dish was a small screwdriver, which was quickly transferred to Queen's pocket.

"The plot thickens!" he said. "I feel like one of the Cato Street conspirators. Sit down and have some dinner," he continued.

Miss Moses sat down. Then Queen asked her to pour out his beer; then she dropped the tumbler, and broke it; then they both went down on their knees to pick up the pieces which had fallen under the table; then the cloth got pulled on one side, and the knives and forks fell off with a crash; then they got things straight again, and went on with their dinner.

Queen got very talkative over the sherry. He began to think a prison, with Miss Moses as a gaoler, was not a bad kind of place, after all.

"I wish I hadn't to go out before to-night," said Queen. "If that fellow Mandarin wasn't coming here at nine o'clock with his confounded *post obit*, I wouldn't."

It was beginning to get dusk when Queen said this, and his gaoler began to hint to him that now or never was his time to escape.

Miss Moses got up, and began to clear away the dishes, and set the room straight.

"He wants a cigar," she said to her mother, when she went into the kitchen.

"Let him have it then," was the reply; "and put it down in the bill for eighteenpence."

I am afraid this was an extortion, as it had only cost the worthy woman one penny, it being one of those concoctions of cabbage-leaves steeped in tobacco juice, termed a

"Pickwick;" nevertheless she told her daughter to say it was a real "Havannah;" and like a dutiful child she said so. All the same, Queen did not believe her.

"It's a confounded cabbage-stalk," was his uncomplimentary remark upon it.

"Now," said Miss Moses, "no tricks about that necklace and bracelets, or I'll stop your little game in less than no time."

"Upon my word," said Queen, "it's all right. Honour bright!"

"Well, then, I'll leave you," said Miss Moses. "I'll say I can't abear your nasty smoke."

"Well, good-bye, my dear," said Queen. "You're a reg'lar brick, that you are!"

Then I am afraid he kissed her, but I am not quite sure—I *think* he did.

Directly Miss Moses left the room, Queen bolted the door, and threw his Pickwick into the empty grate. Then he pulled out the screwdriver, and began working away at the bar. Of course it stuck tight, and he could not move it. Here was a fix!—every moment was of importance: it was half-past eight, and Mandarin would be here at nine; he shook the bar, and tried to rock it in its socket, but all to no purpose. "Curse the bar!" he said. "I shall have to sign, after all."

Queen was a powerful man, and his weight soon began to tell on the woodwork, which was rather rotten from age and damp. It began to split and crack round the bottom of the bar.

Just then came a sharp rat-rat at the door, and a voice was heard saying, "Let me in, Queen, old fellow; let me in."

It was Mandarin, and Queen redoubled his efforts. "Wait a minute," he said, "and I'll let you in."

Then he worked frantically at the bar:

it began to give way. Mandarin heard the noise, and beginning to guess the cause, thundered at the door. Luckily for Queen the door was a very strong one, and resisted his efforts; also that the parlour was away from the other parts of the house, so the noise did not attract the notice of the inhabitants.

Miss Moses heard it, but she guessed the cause, and went straightway to her piano, and played the " Battle of Prague," to try and drown it.

She succeeded perfectly ; her father and mother were in the kitchen below, and heard her.

"Mariar do play luv'ly," said Mrs. Moses to her spouse. " Do you hear the drums and cannons a rolling?"

" She's making a beastly row," said the sheriff's-officer, who had no soul for music.

"I call it luv'ly," said his wife.

"And I don't," he replied, puffing at his clay churchwarden. "And if I'd a known what it would come to, I'd never a paid for her learning the piany at the boardin'-school—that I wouldn't."

The drums and cannons of the poetic imagination of Mrs. Moses was Major Mandarin thundering at Queen's door.

Meanwhile the prisoner worked might and main: at last, away came the bar with a crash. Queen dragged the table-cloth off and knotted it round one of the others, and swung himself out on to the leads.

"By Jove, it's like a scene in one of Boucicault's plays!" said Queen, as he swung to the ground.

The noise got so loud and furious that Mr. Moses threw down his pipe and said, "I'll go and put a stopper on that gal's pianer playing — it's unbearable!"

Then he went up to the "parler," where Miss Moses was playing the "Battle of Prague" with great energy.

"Hold yer row, gal, *do*," said her father. "Give over! we've had enough of it. Burn the piany!" he said, giving the instrument a kick. "I wish I hadn't been such a fool as to give it to you!"

The knocks still went on.

"Then it ain't the piany!" said Mr. Moses, staring at it with astonishment, "unless it goes of hisself, which I think he do sometimes."

"By Jove, it's the 'bird!'" he exclaimed, and flew up the passage.

"What the devil are you making such a row about?" he hallooed, as he ran.

When he got to the door he stumbled over the Major.

" He's got out of window!" said Mandarin. "Get round to the back of the house and nab him."

Mr. Moses flew down the back stairs, and flung open the door leading on to the leads. There was not a trace of his prisoner to be seen; nothing but the table-cloth hanging to the bar.

Major Mandarin joined him on the leads. " You'll have to pay this, you know," he said. " It's a case of two thousand pounds."

Mr. Moses turned pale. " I haven't got two thousand pence in the world," he said, piteously, " much less pounds!"

" I don't care whether you've got it or not," said the Major. " I mean to have it, and you must find it!"

" Have mercy on me!" said Moses. " I can't pay it. I can't, indeed."

" Do you think your daughter knows anything about it?" said Mandarin.

"If she does I'll break every bone in her body," said her fond father; "the hussy!"

"Don't do that," said the Major. "Leave her to me. I'll soon find out whether she knows anything or not."

"All right, sir," said Moses, only too glad to please the Major in any way. "I know my father's feelin's might prevent me doing my duty by her!"

Then they both went into the house. Mrs. Moses was crying on the stairs, keeping up a kind of duet with the maid, who was doing it out of sympathy for her mistress.

"Oh! Abram, here's a go!" said Mrs. Moses.

"Hold yer row!" replied her husband. "Where's the gal?"

"In there!" replied his wife, pointing to the parlour.

"Good evening, Miss," said Mandarin, when he went in.

Miss Moses was sitting on the music-stool, thumping the piano.

"So your bird has flown?" he said.

"Yes, poor gentleman!" she replied, "he has. Liberty is sweet!"

"Did he pine much?" said the Major, tenderly.

"Awful, sir!" said Miss Moses.

"Was he morose or affable," inquired Mandarin.

"First he was one, then he was the other," she replied.

"Which was he at last?" said Mandarin.

"H'affable," said Miss Moses.

"Did you see much of Lord Henry?" asked the Major.

"I had my bit of dinner with the poor gentleman. He said it cheered him up!"

"Good night, Miss," said the Major; then he left the room.

"If that gal hadn't a hand in it, I'm a Dutchman," he said to himself as he went out. Then he went to his own place with the naughty name, and fleeced Spooner out of his half-year's salary, which he lent him again at twenty-five per cent.

When Queen dropped down on to the leads, he made the best of his way over the roof of the mews, and then clambered down a waterspout. "There'll be a hue and cry," he said to himself; "I must cut and run."

Queen had a pound or two in his pocket, so he went down to the London Bridge Wharf, and embarked on board one of the steam-packets for Boulogne. By one o'clock in the morning the vessel was fairly under way for "la belle France," with Lord Henry Fitzreine on board, amongst a miscellaneous cargo of commercial gents, old women, babies, and mossoos.

Oh! that dreadful Nore!

But we discreetly drop a curtain over the harrowing scene, and merely wish them "Bon voyage!"

CHAPTER III.

ROTTEN ROW.

"You have too much respect upon the world.
They lose it, that do buy it with much care."
SHAKSPEARE.

F any one wishes to see a full assemblage of "worldlings," let them go to the "Row" at one P.M., any day in the season. There they all are—peers, M.P.'s, duchesses, bishops, and Traviatas, all jumbled up together for the space of an hour in the middle of the day. The great goddess Fashion has decreed that so it shall be, and accordingly so it is: she is a very despot to her votaries.

Lady George was sitting on one of the chairs; as usual, she had a little knot of men round her. Belgravian mothers said she was a "leetle" fast, but then she was so well-connected that it made up for it in their eyes, as it makes up for anything.

"I hope my theatricals wont turn out a failure?" she said to Stapleton.

"Nothing you undertake can fail to be a success," was his polite rejoinder.

"Gammon!" said Lady George. "I make young mulls, like other people."

"I wonder if it is very difficult to act," said Stapleton. "I think I should like it, if it's pretty easy."

"Easy!" exclaimed Lady George; "it's as easy as lying!"

"Well, it is *not* difficult then," said Stapleton, "for most people can do that at a pinch."

"Put me out of your catalogue," said

Lady George; "I wouldn't tell a lie to save my life."

I am afraid Lady George extolled her virtue too high here. I have caught her out once or twice; but then, to be sure, they were only *white* ones, and " worldlings" say that *they* are not lies at all, only equivocations. I will say that she did not mean to tell a lie, only her code was not a very strict one—at least, not up to the mark of Curseum Chapel.

"I have got quite a new thing in the shape of a play," said Lady George. "Charlie has adapted 'La belle Hélène' for drawing-room performance, and it will be quite a novelty to the B. P. off the stage!"

"That's what the young fool has been scribbling in his room, then," said Stapleton. "We all thought it was an 'Ode to a Snowdrop,' or something of that sort. One of 'ours' made a few stanzas, and sent it to him by post, purporting to have been written by himself."

"Let's hear it," said Lady George.

"Here it is," replied Stapleton.

"TO A SNOWDROP.

" Fairest primeval of Spring,
An offering to your bower I bring.
Nearer to approach I can't,
By reason of your dragon-aunt,
Who looks with no favouring eyes
Upon my prayers, my tears, my sighs!
Wilt thou, wilt thou fly with me
To realms of love beyond the sea?
Where *I* shall gaze with rapture on your charms,
And *both* be happy in each other's arms!"

"Bravo!" said Lady George; "the fellow who made that is a trump."

"*I* wrote it," said Stapleton, looking pleased and gratified.

"Did you *really?*" said Lady George. "Who'd have thought it of you?"

Just then Fitzcharles came up.

"Good morning," said Lady George. "How go the preparations in Curzon

Street? Have you arranged about the footlights?"

"It's all right," he replied. "They came with the rest of the things, at the same time as the portable theatre."

"I am always in a fuss when I've got people coming," said Lady George. "I say, Charlie," she continued, "so you've been writing an 'Ode to a Snowdrop.' 'Fairest primeval of Spring,'" she began.

"I didn't write it," he replied. "One of the fellows did, and sent it to me by post."

"Oh, it's all very well!" said Lady George. "They express your sentiments just as if you had done it yourself."

"Perhaps they do," said Fitzcharles, ruefully, as he took the next chair to Lady George.

"Why don't you 'cut and run' to Gretna Green," said Lady George, "or whatever answers to the same purpose in these days?"

"Because I don't see *how* we are to be married," he replied. "Because I can't get a licence without swearing I and Minnie are both of age. And I don't like swearing to a lie!"

"Hire one of the 'supers' at 'Her Highness's,'" said Lady George, "and dress him in a frock-coat, and make him look respectable. The people at Doctors' Commons will think he's your father."

"By Jove, so they would!" he replied. "I never thought of that."

"Or run over to Paris for a fortnight, and then come back and get whitewashed by Whitey Brown," her ladyship continued.

"I don't like to ask Minnie to do that," said Fitzcharles, "because the world would say such ill-natured things of her. I don't care what they say about me, but I shouldn't like them to talk about *her*."

"Rubbish!" said Lady George; "let them say what they like. I believe the mutual allegiance of two hearts, which have solemnly sworn to be faithful to each other before heaven, is as pure and holy a marriage in the sight of God as if it had taken place at St. George's, Hanover Square, under the auspices of the Archbishop of Canterbury, assisted by a dozen 'honourable and reverends,' with a cloud of bridesmaids! I'd just as soon be married gipsy-fashion, by jumping over a broomstick, as with a full choral service. I think marriage is a civil and earthly contract, which, as Christians, we ought to consecrate by asking the blessing of God upon it. But, *per se*, it is not a religious contract. The *ceremony* itself is not a sacrament—he *marriage* is."

N.B.—These are Lady George's sentiments, *not* the author's. Her ladyship is not orthodox on *all* points—I am. I have allowed these remarks of Lady George's to go to the press rather with a view of advancing some arguments against an idea very prevalent in this age of free-thinking, and, if possible, to show cause *why* a marriage should be solemnized by a religious ceremony. Some people may think that the subject should not be entered into at all; but I am convinced that erroneous ideas often take deep root from not being sufficiently ventilated. Right views are all the more strongly developed from looking at the wrong side of the question as well. I, for one, believe in the teaching of contrasts. Show a man a black-clad devil and a white-robed angel, he will prefer the latter. But show him a lot of drab-coloured nondescripts, and he wont know which to choose from, because they are all so much alike, there is no force of contrast. I am not prepared, *prima facie*, to adjudicate that Lady George is hopelessly and irrecoverably wrong; or to deny that a marriage in a register-office, or a Scotch marriage, is not as valid in the Court of Heaven as if the ceremony was solemnized in a Church. But what I *do* say is, destroy the sanctity of the marriage tie, and you open wide the floodgates of profligacy and libertinism, and sap the very foundations of society. Besides, does not His presence at the marriage in Cana of Galilee convey some teaching with it, and shed a halo over the rite for all time, and point to the Church as the fittest place wherein to ratify such solemn vows, and, as it were, *consecrate* the most important epoch in our lives by the offices of religion? There should be something very defined to mark the pure espousals of a Christian man and woman from the chains of lust on the one part, and greed for gold on the other, which unite for a time a man of loose principles and a harlot.

"I am very wretched and miserable," said Fitzcharles: then the tears began to trickle down his cheeks.

"Don't be so down in the mouth," said Lady George. "It will come all right in the end. You are going to act 'Paris' to-night, and she's your 'belle Hélène.' By Jove!" continued Lady George, "make a reality of the thing—elope after the play's over. It will be a glorious finale to my party and the London season!"

"I only wish I could!" said Fitzcharles, ruefully.

"*Could!* you stupid boy! Why you can," said Lady George. "She'll do it in a minute. Any girl who's worth anything is game for an elopement at a moment's notice. Besides, there is a touch of romance in the whole thing. Two friendless orphans; a dreadful dragon of an aunt; and a sympathizing, beneficent old woman (that's me). You *must* do it to-morrow night, or I shall be quite angry with both of you."

"If Minnie will, I will," he replied.

"Of course she will," said Lady George; "that is, if she cares about you. Any girl who *really* cares about a fellow would. I shall be quite annoyed if my party doesn't end with Paris and Hélène *really* making themselves scarce—it will be such fun. I quite long for to-morrow!"

Just then Sir John Fenacre came up with Madeleine leaning on his arm.

"Good morning, Lady George," he said. "I have been looking for you everywhere, but there is such a crush one can't see anybody."

Then he took his seat on a vacant chair on the other side of Lady George. When he had settled himself, he said, in a low voice, "Have you given that woman her money?"

"No!" said Lady George.

"Why not?" said Sir John.

"Because she's dead," she replied.

"Good heavens!" he exclaimed, "how sudden. I shan't have to pay the money now."

"Yes you will," said Lady George.

"Why?" he replied.

"Because there are three children."

"Let 'em go into the workhouse," said the Baronet; "I wont keep them."

"You forget our conversation at the opera?" said Lady George.

"You really are too bad; you're like a trade-unionist!" said Sir John. "I suppose I must go on with it then?"

"Certainly," said Lady George. "Next Monday again, please."

"The Duchess has asked us down to Scotland for the 12th of August, so I mean to postpone our continental tour," said Sir John.

"I am going down too," said Lady George. "I hate being at Inverness, but I never know what to do in August if I don't go abroad."

"The Duchess seems awfully cut up about Lord Henry," said Sir John.

"Dagenham told me this morning that he gave the bailiffs the slip; let himself out of window by a table-cloth. There was a petticoat in the business, I believe," said Lady George.

"As in most," said the Baronet.

"They traced him down to London Bridge, and they suppose he went on board one of the Boulogne packets."

"Very likely," said Sir John.

Before he was "Sir" John, he had fled to Boulogne himself—the Philistines in hot pursuit. If foreigners were to judge of England and the English by specimens of the Saxon race they see at Boulogne, our character would not stand very high in the estimation of Europe.

Fortunately this is not the case.

"Whose suit was he arrested at?" asked Sir John.

"Oh! a fellow named Mandarin, *alias* Pluto," replied her ladyship.

"What does the Duke say to the business?" said Sir John.

"Oh! he swears he wont pay a farthing of the money," said Lady George; "and what's put him out more than anything is an anonymous letter this morning, saying Henry had signed a *post obit* on him before he left."

"Enough to put any man out!" said the Baronet.

"Yes," replied Lady George, "because he's always been so liberal to him, that it naturally 'riles' him. He swears he'd cut him off with a shilling if he could. Luckily for poor Henry, his money is secured in his mother's settlement, so he cannot carry out his threat if he would."

"That's lucky for him," said Sir John; "because when the Duke once says he'll do a thing, he does it."

"I like him for that," said Lady George. "If a dog growls and barks, I like him to bite—at least, *other* people, of course."

"Of course," re-echoed the Baronet.

Sir John and Lady George were on very intimate terms, as we have seen by their conversation. They were connected in a sort of way through her sister, Lady Fenacre, so they discussed their mutual family affairs as relations—in fact, with rather more freedom than relatives would have used towards each other. Lady George took a pleasure in finding out people's private affairs: all about their income, expectations, flirtations, quarrels, and family feuds; in return, she was always ready to regale the retailers of general gossip with highly-spiced anecdotes of her husband's family, the Maldons; and I am afraid the character of that noble house rather suffered by her revelations.

"It's a case of give and take," Lady George said.

If you want to know other people's affairs, you must tell them something about your own or your family's; the latter is the best, because no one but a fool makes the world his father-confessor! Apropos of gossiping, there is a vast difference in it. There are two sorts—ill-natured and harmless. The former retails stories to the disadvantage of people, seriously affecting their characters; the latter laughs good-naturedly at their foibles and follies! What a dull world it would be if we did not laugh at our neighbours! If we abstain from conscientious scruples, we may be quite sure our neighbours have *not* these scruples, and are continually indulging in a jest at our expense. It is the way of the world to laugh at one another, and if it is done *good-naturedly*, it is a very harmless amusement.

Lady George got tired of talking to Sir John, and began to stare, and criticise the " worldlings," who were prancing up and down, some on horses, and a great number on their ten toes.

In a half-hour in the " Row" you see a greater variety of character than in any other place in the same given time. There is the country cousin who is for the day to see the glories of the town, and has left

Cambridgeshire early in the morning, while the fog is still hanging on the marshes, and got into London before the inhabitants are well out of bed and breakfasted. He cools his superfluous energy amongst the Elgin marbles in the British Museum; then he goes by the Underground to Baker Street and sees the waxworks; then he goes on to the Park. He is painfully conscious that he is not so spruce as the "worldlings," who have only walked in from Mayfair, and therefore have not turned a hair; he, on the contrary, being rather travel-stained in his journey westwards from the wilds of Shoreditch. However, he pulls out his primrose-coloured kid gloves, till now carefully concealed in his pocket, and puts a bold face on the matter, and jostles up and down the crowd with the best. Then he meets some of his town acquaintances, and other country cousins like himself, and really enjoys himself, while the languid "worldlings" doze and yawn that the "Wow is a hawid bor!" Then there is the country parson and his daughters. "Pa" is in town for the "May Meetings" (which are oftener held in June), and he has brought Mary and Jane into the Park to see the fashionable world. The poor girls are painfully aware that their "get-up" is awfully dowdy, and their bonnets are of a fearfully antiquated pattern. They envy the gorgeous apparel of Traviata—they wouldn't, if they knew what she was—they think she is a Duchess or a Countess at the very least, by her dress. "Pa" has no feeling for them with regard to their dress. "As long as you have got a good gown, what's it matter if it's one shape or another?" are his sentiments. Mary and Jane think otherwise, and are nearly ready to cry with vexation about their "things." All these and many more varieties of the *genus homo* may be seen any day in the "Row" during the season.

The Duke of Maldon was riding in the Park on a roan-coloured horse: he looked very grim, morose, and sulky. He was thinking about the *post obit.* "The ungrateful dog!" he muttered between his teeth, as he entered the ride through the posts at "the corner."

Then he started off at a good canter towards the Knightsbridge end of the Row. He flogged and spurred his horse most unmercifully during his progress. He was naturally a "merciful man to his beast," but he was thoroughly in a rage, and felt he must vent it on *some one.* Every time he struck his horse he thought, "I wish it was Henry;" then he redoubled his blows. Coachmen have this same feeling. If one of the fraternity are in a rage with their employers, they vent it on the unoffending horses. A duke is but mortal, and does the same.

Before his Grace left Grosvenor Square, he had vented his wrath on his wife in words, but he could not hurt and strike her, therefore it gave him a kind of grim satisfaction to punish his horse. By the time he had been up and down the ride a few times, he was quite in a good humour with *himself*, and not ill-disposed toward mankind in general. Directly he left home, the Duchess of Maldon had fastened upon her niece Miss Snowdrop, bullied her till she cried, and then sent her up to her room. Then she sat down to write notes with a smiling face; her wrath had found a safety-valve, and had evaporated, for a time, like steam from a boiler!

The Duke reined in his horse before the railings opposite Lady George's chair: his daughter-in-law got up to speak to him.

"Confounded nuisance, this affair of Henry's!" said his Grace, working himself up into a rage. Then he struck his horse violently and reined it up sharp, under the delusive idea that it would not stand still. This caused a slight rebellion on the part of the much-enduring quadruped, which was quelled with stern measures immediately.

"I shouldn't care about the money, only I hate him specking on my death," continued his Grace.

"Perhaps he hasn't done it?" said Lady George. "The letter was only anonymous."

"I am afraid it's only too true," he replied. "The man in possession of the papers offered to send them for my inspection."

"He only wants you to buy them up,' said Lady George.

"Then he wont get what he wants," said

the Duke, striking his horse, "for I don't mean to give Henry another farthing as long as I live!"

"I shouldn't believe it without inquiry," said Lady George. "Why don't you let Parchment see the papers?"

"I think I will," said the Duke. "The ungrateful dog!" he exclaimed, apostrophizing his son, and at the same time administering corporal punishment to his horse. "I must be off now," he continued. "I'm going to have luncheon at the Fogies."

"You'll be sure and come to-night?" said Lady George.

"Oh yes!" he replied. "I wont forget. I shouldn't like to miss your party."

"Thank you," replied her ladyship; "I feel flattered."

Then the Duke rode down to the Fogies, in St. James's Street, and Lady George went back to her chair.

The crowd was thinning, and people were going home to luncheon. Lady George asked a few "fellows" she happened to see, to come to her house that night for the theatricals; then she got into her brougham, which was waiting for her near the "corner," and went home.

Sir John and Madeleine went back to the Clarendon, and Stapleton and Fitzcharles went back to luncheon at the mess of their regiment—the Life Guards Green, which is not a hundred miles from the open-air "Fops' Alley," in Hyde Park.

A mess luncheon is a kind of phœnix that has emerged from the ashes of breakfast; for one is not over before the other begins. The "gallant commanders" of the Life Guards Green were indulging in cooling compounds, such as shandygaff and claret-cup from out of shining silver tankards, presented to the regiment by former brothers-in-arms.

There is no atmosphere so congenial to "chaff" as mess-rooms. All the "fellows" get it without mercy, especially the subs. Sometimes there is an old captain who has not been able to purchase, and is stranded amongst his juniors. If he has any peculiarities (and who has not?), he gets it with tenfold force. "Have you heard Slowcoach's last?" asks a gallant "Green." "No," you reply. "Oh! Fitzbattleaxe asked him whether he was fond of dancing, and he replied, 'Oh! *passionately*, but *not* with women!' Who the deuce *would* the fellow dance with, I should like to know? Whenever he goes to a ball now, we ask him whether he danced with a woman or a donkey? 'Both,' he always says. Slowcoach doesn't care much about the sex; he thinks them a horrid bore."

Directly Fitzcharles got into the room, Fitzbattleaxe got up, and with a mock heroic and tragical air, began to recite :

> " Fairest primeval of Spring,
> An offering to your bower I bring."

There was a roar of laughter round the table, and the poor youth sat down, blushing from the roots of his hair to the tips of his little toes!

> " Nearer to approach I can't,
> By reason of your dragon-aunt "—

continued Fitzbattleaxe, amidst a perfect hurricane of laughter.

> " Who looks with no favouring eyes
> Upon my prayers, my tears, my sighs.
> Wilt thou, wilt thou fly with me
> To realms of love beyond the sea ?
> When *I* can gaze with rapture on your charms,
> And *both* be happy in each other's arms !"

" Bravo, Fitz !" shouted the fellows. " Encore! encore!" then they thundered on the table.

Fitzbattleaxe bowed with gravity, after the fashion of a popular actor acknowledging the plaudits of the house, and then sat down.

Poor Fitzcharles could not stand it any longer; he *nearly* cried; he had to save his manhood by rushing off to his room, amidst derisive shouts of laughter, and the chorus of "Fairest primeval of Spring."

When he did get to his room, he threw himself on his bed and *did* cry. He could not help it—he really could not.

However, he soon dried his tears, and went to the Colonel's quarters to ask for leave. This he got without any trouble; Colonel Sabretache, of the Life Guards Green, was no martinet.

"All right, my boy!" he said; "but I don't understand you wanting to go away in the middle of the season. I hope you are not up to any mischief."

Poor Charlie blushed and stammered, and said nothing.

"Oh, you are a sad young dog!" said his Colonel. "But boys will be boys; so take your leave, and be —— to you!"

This was his grim style of pleasantry.

CHAPTER IV.

LADY GEORGE'S THEATRICALS.

"All the world's a stage,
And all the men and women merely players."
SHAKSPEARE.

LADY GEORGE'S house in Curzon Street was in the state termed "upside down;" the drawing-rooms were being cleared, and the portable theatre, with its complete adjuncts of side-scenes, wings, and footlights, was being erected in the back room. There were folding-doors between the two, but these had been taken off their hinges and carried off to the lower regions. All the furniture had been consigned to the same place, and a number of red velvet and gilt fauteuils substituted for the usual sofas, lounging-chairs, and general bijouteries, with which the room was always crammed.

Lady George herself was sitting in her own private boudoir, expecting her *dramatis personæ* for the final rehearsal, which was to take place in her sanctum. On ordinary occasions none but her most privileged familiars were admitted there; she liked keeping a room which was emphatically *her own*—a room of which having once shut the door, she was secure from all intrusion.

It is very pleasant to have a *den* sacred to oneself, especially if you are blessed with a numerous circle of relatives, all residing under the same roof as yourself.

There was *one* individual who went in and out at his pleasure; that we need hardly say was her ladyship's son, Master Charles, whose infantile gambols, and unwarrantable freedom with Jay's "moke;" we have witnessed.

Lady George was sitting by the window reading a novel. "What bosh!" she exclaimed, as she threw down the book. "These novels are all alike; a *pièce de résistance* of murder, with a *sauce piquante à l'adultère*; reliefs of bigamy, and *entrées* of illegitimate children! They're all alike, every one of them!"

"How *can* you talk like that, Lily?" said Lady Fenacre, who was sitting with her sister.

"It's quite true," she replied; "and as that's the case, why shouldn't I say so?"

Lady George was *not* of the number of those who call a spade an agricultural implement. The modern novel *is* precisely what her ladyship described it, and therefore why should not she say so? There is an abundance of prudish, false delicacy in the world, which calls ugly things by pretty names; then it is all right. But call a spade a spade in these days, and you have a chorus of "Fies!" upon you at once. You are set down immediately as a very "improper" person, and one who says very *gauche* things.

"I am glad my theatricals will be different to other people's," said Lady George. "Fancy going-in for the classical in a drawing-room! It will be something quite new, and that's what I like. I hate going on in the old groove my grandmother hewed out for herself. Why should I, I should like to know?"

Why, indeed, are we to follow the track of our worthy progenitors? Let each one hew out a path for himself or herself, as the case may be.

We need not be like "dumb, driven cattle," though very few of us are "heroes in the strife," in spite of Mr. Longfellow's exhortation.

Fitzcharles' version of "La Belle Hélène" was not much like the original, except with regard to the finale of the elopement of Paris and Helen. He took the same freedom with the classics that H. J. Byron and the other burlesque writers do, insomuch that, except in the name, it bore no resemblance whatever to what is told us of the freaks of the gods and goddesses with mortals, by Homer and other worthies.

There were to be three scenes. The first was to be in the temple of the Delphian oracle, where Paris was to consult the priestess of Venus, as to where he should find the most beautiful girl for his wife. The second was to be a happy valley in Arcadia, when Venus was to appear to Helen and her attendant maidens, and warn her that the Great Jove "had his eye on her," and that she, the goddess, would befriend her. The third and last was to be the arrival of Paris in Arcadia, when after the usual amount of love-making, including a duel with the Great Jove, king of the gods, and other minor circumstances, he was to bear off in triumph "la belle Hélène," to dwell for ever in bliss and felicity.

This is a short sketch of the plot, which was written expressly for Lady George Fitzreine's theatricals, which took place at the end of the season of 186—, and were memorable in the annals of the fashionable world, till they found something else to talk about, which was not long.

All the dresses were arranged on chairs round the room, and Lady George got up to write out the play-bills on her own monogrammed paper. For the information of the readers of "Fenacre Grange," we will give the "cast" *verbatim*, which means, or is supposed to mean, precisely as her ladyship wrote them.

The following is a true and correct copy:

CURZON STREET. June —, 186—.

"*The Ugly Jove and La Belle Hélène.*"

Jove. (King of the Gods, and the terror of mortals, who is very much in love with la belle Hélène.) . . . Algernon Fitzbattleaxe.

Æsculapius. (God of Physic, and Jove's factotum.)
Loftus Fenacre.

Paris. (A love-sick youth, who is a devout votary of Venus.) . . . . Charles Fitzcharles.

La Belle Hélène. (An Arcadian nymph, who is cruelly persecuted by Jove, whose attentions she rejects with scorn; but has no objection to other people's.) . Hon. Miss Snowdrop.

Venus. (Goddess of Beauty and Queen of Love, who, notwithstanding her heavenly origin, has a *penchant* for mortal men.) . Miss Fenacre.

Pythia. (Priestess of Delphi, and devoted to the service of Venus, whose back-hair she does daily) . . . . Lady George Fitzbeine.

Lady George wrote about fifty of these bills. "There!" she exclaimed, "I wont write any more; people must look at each other's. I'm sick of the whole thing already. I was a fool not to have them printed. If it wasn't for the *finale* I should hate the whole concern. If that girl hangs fire, I'll never speak to her again, or help her out of her rows with the old woman."

The "characters" began to drop in one by one. The first arrival was Madeleine Fenacre. Lady George went up and kissed her, and made her sit down on the sofa by her side.

Girls kiss each other before the other sex, with the hope that the men will inwardly wish it was them. Women kissing one another is like the conference of the spies. They have a smile on their faces and war in their hearts. It is not a sign of affection with them, only a conventionality—a case of what is termed " kiss your face and cut your throat" love. Another peculiarity of their sex is to have " *she*-lovers." This is principally confined to school-girls, and young ladies who despair of ever having a *he* one.

All the *dramatis personæ* having assembled, Lady George moved a resolution to the effect that they should go through their parts. This was carried *nem. con.*

The last rehearsal is always rather a nervous thing for amateur performers. There is always *some one* who does not know his part; and, what is more, does not seem likely to when the scratch comes. In this case the delinquent was the Great Jove, king of the gods, &c. He did not know a word of it.

"I wish people would learn their part," said Lady George; "that is, if they are not too stupid!"

She was in a rage, and said it *at* Fitzbattleaxe. There never was, and never will be, a piece performed without a vast amount of preliminary bickering on the part of the actors and actresses. It is human nature, and will be so for all time. Then they had a picnic luncheon in Lady George's boudoir, and got very merry and cheerful over the sherry.

Those scramble luncheons are much more sociable and informal than all sitting, looking at one another, round the table; though if they were to occur too often, we should sigh for a mahogany and a dining-room chair.

About three o'clock the party dispersed, all promising to meet again at nine, sharp- During the luncheon, arrangements were made between two of the party, which had no connexion with the evening's entertainment—at least, it remained to be proved whether people would be entertained by it or not. But of this more hereafter.

Lady George went for a drive in the Park at five, then she went to Grosvenor Square, and dined, *en famille*, with the noble house of Maldon.

The dinner party was as usual anything but pleasant, owing to the antagonistic propensities of the race of Fitzreine. That noble family habitually contradicted one another during soup; "slanged" one another when the fish came; and, at the *pièce de résistance*, they were usually in the midst of a row-royal. When it had reached its height, it generally subsided, but only gradually, like a thunder-storm. An ominous growl would remind you that the tempest was not *quite* over, or, at least, was always ready to burst out again at the slightest provocation.

Queen's escapade had not mended matters in this respect. The *post obit* stuck in the Duke's throat like a fish-bone: it would neither come up or go down—it remained just where it was. Their eldest son and heir-presumptive to the honours of the ducal house of Maldon, Viscount Dagenham, was dining with them. He was afflicted, as we already know, with fits. Both his parents thought he would never live, so they had rather transferred the "eldest son" feeling of affection to Henry, their second son; George, the third brother, died soon after his marriage, as we all know.

Since his brother's flight to Boulogne, he had been rather "taken up" by the Duke and Duchess. Those German baths did wonders sometimes; and who knows what they might do in his case? All these things made Dagenham in high favour in Grosvenor Square.

The Duke was naturally more irate about the *post obit* than the Duchess, because it was "done" on him, not her. Henry was her favourite son, and, as we have seen, she had laid deep plans for his matrimonial happiness. But now, as Dagenham was so much better, Sir John Fenacre would not be so complacent, of course; and especially on account of those disagreeable disclosures with reference to Henry's finances, which had just been published to the world. She determined, however, inwardly annoyed and miserable as she was, to go to Lady George's theatricals. " I am not going to have the world pitying *me*," she said, "and shrugging their shoulders out of sympathy, and retailing to each other that I am sitting at home, crying. I mean to go about as if nothing had happened, and brave them all."

This was why she was going to witness the burlesque of " Jove and la belle Hélène" in Curzon Street. At half-past eight Lady George's brougham came to fetch her: she did not keep it waiting, and went home, taking Miss Snowdrop with her.

" Well, my dear," said Lady George, when they were both in the carriage, " how do you feel?"

"Very frightened," she replied.

"Rubbish! What is there to be frightened at? I suppose you love him, and all that sort of thing?"

"Love him!" said Miss Snowdrop; "of course I do!"

"Then, for heaven's sake, don't make a fool of yourself," said Lady George. "You'll put me in a rage if you do." Then Lady George kissed her, to make amends for her seemingly harsh speech.

Of course it was very wrong of Lady George to take an elopement under her wing in this way; but then people do not *always* do what they ought, not even "respectable" people!

Lady George found Jove, Æsculapius, Venus, and Paris, all in her drawing-room, though as yet in their ordinary habiliments. The stage was erected in the back drawing-room; both the rooms were lit by sunlights, and everything looked very pretty. There was to be dancing after the play, so the carpet was up, and red cloth put down in lieu thereof, till it should commence.

"We'd better all go and dress," said Lady George. Then she rang for a servant to show the heathen deities their dressing-rooms, and carried off Venus and la belle Hélène to her own.

Venus, of course, did not know that the elopement was to be a reality, notwithstanding her celestial wisdom.

Lady Fenacre remained down in the drawing-room to receive the guests, who by ten o'clock had nearly all arrived and were packed in their places. An orchestra, consisting of five or six men belonging to the band of the Life Guards Green, was arranged in a wing at the side of the stage.

The overture commenced: it was an air selected from Offenbach's opera, on which the little *vaudeville* about to be performed was a burlesque. This over, the rooms were suddenly darkened, and the curtain rose to slow music. It disclosed an alcove in the Temple of Delphi, in which was an altar, and over it, suspended in a bronze dish by three chains, the sacred fire.

There was a burst of applause when the curtain reached its last fold: every one said they had never seen anything like it in a private house.

Pythia was discovered sitting on a low stool by the altar, with her face buried in her arms, and great wavy masses of light-brown hair flowing down her back. She was dressed in a long robe of white cashmere, fastened at the waist by a gold girdle in the shape of a serpent; other gold serpents were coiled round her neck and arms, and she had a gold coronet on her head, and on her feet gilt sandals, without any stockings.

There was a continued round of applause, amongst which Stapleton's "bravo" could be plainly distinguished.

Then Pythia rose up and chanted a hymn in praise of Venus; this over, Paris entered to consult the oracle. Paris was dressed very splendidly in gold and spangles, and, by his own confession to the priestess, had got everything he wanted but a wife. This want Pythia undertook to supply if he would make an offering to her patron Venus. Paris threw a purse on to the altar, and then proceeded to strike a bargain. This concluded, he retired again. After his exit, Venus appeared in a rose-coloured cloud to her priestess, and spying the purse on the altar, immediately pocketed it. She was attired in a blue silk, of classical cut, over a white silk dress, and looked her part. She told her priestess, in a kind of doggrel rhyme, of Jove's partiality for a mortal called la belle Hélène, and her determination to frustrate his designs. This over, she disappeared in the same rose-coloured cloud; and the curtain went down amidst vociferous shouts and tumultuous applause.

Then all the people began to discuss the merits of the piece in no very cynical spirit.

"I wish Lily hadn't got her feet bare," said the Duchess to Lady Mountchessington, who was sitting next to her. "I think it's hardly decent."

"*Everything's* decent now," replied her ladyship.

"What pretty feet Lily's got," said the Duke to his wife.

"I don't see it," she replied.

"Because you're jealous," he said, *sotto voce*. His wife pretended she did not hear him.

Then the curtain went up again, and the

band played softly. A group of children came in, dancing in time to it, and scattering flowers as they went along. Then came the heroine of the piece, Hélène, who took her seat in a bower of roses; then the children danced a little ballet, seemingly for her edification only, but in reality for that of the spectators. This over, Venus appeared to her, and told her that a lover was even now swimming across the Hellespont to her, like Leander, and that eventually she would marry him, in spite of the machinations of the Great Jove.

Then the curtain fell for the second time, and the band struck up a lively air.

"How pretty your niece looks!" said Lady Mountchessington.

"It's very good of you to say so; but I cannot say I think it: she's so frightfully awkward and *gauche*."

Up went the curtain again for the last

scene; Paris and Hélène were discovered making fierce love in the bower of roses, whilst Jove, attended by Æsculapius, is listening behind the bushes. Jove, greatly irate, asks Æsculapius what is to be done to put a stop to such folly? " Calomel," replies the sage, pulling out a phial of it. They both advanced to the front; Paris discovers them, and rushes out with drawn sword. A duel ensues on the triangular principle, amidst the tears of la belle Hélène. At length Venus appears, followed by Pythia, and Hélène implores her aid. This the goddess grants, and steps between the combatants. Jove yields to the almighty power of love, and falls, fainting, into the arms of his second, Æsculapius. During his " coming to," Paris and Hélène elope, by means of an argosy bound for Illyria, in which a passage has been secured for them by direction of Venus. When Jove recovered, Venus read him a lesson on the power of love, which concluded with the lines out of Walter Scott's "Marmion":—

> " Love rules the court, the camp, the grove,
> Men below and saints above :
> For love is heaven, and heaven is love."

Then the curtain fell finally, and a perfect roar of applause rose from the audience. The excitement for a few minutes was intense, every one was talking at once. " It was the best thing they had ever seen; there wasn't a hitch anywhere." The Duke was red in the face with pride, as person after person came up and congratulated him on the success of his daughter's theatricals—there had been nothing like it since the old days at Carlton House!

" If the truth was known, I daresay Paris is kissing Helen behind the scenes," said the Duchess to her husband. " She's a forward girl !"

"Let'em!" said his Grace. He was brimful of good-humour and the milk of human kindness, and had a glow of complacency on his face. If you had asked him for fifty pounds at that moment he would have given it. It is at such moments as these that we think the round world and they that dwell therein a tip-top concern, and are glad we are in it.

There was a general move for the supper-room, and for an hour an incessant popping of champagne-corks was kept up. Lady George was not long before she appeared amongst her guests, dressed in white *moiré*, with red flowers and silver cord in her hair. She was literally *assailed* with congratulations on all sides.

Madeleine was not long before she followed her. She came into the room with the *ci-devant* Æsculapius; she wore white silk with black ornaments.

During supper the room had been cleared

for dancing, and the band arranged on the stage, which had been so lately sacred to the mythologies. The Duchess was peering round the room with her eye-glass, looking for her niece.

"Where's Minnie?" she said to Lady George, who happened to stop just opposite to her during a pause in a waltz she was doing with Fitzbattleaxe.

"Perhaps she's gone to lie down," replied her ladyship: "she said she was tired." Then she went on dancing.

"I hope she is," said the Duchess, charitably. "And I should like to know where that young fool is. I daresay he's sitting with her. I'll go and put a stop to *that!*"

Then she rose up and searched the house; she went into every corner, and could not find her. She came back to the ball-room, and communicated the result of her expedition to Lady George.

"Perhaps she's gone home," said her ladyship. "With two hundred people here, I have other things to do besides looking after her."

"Perhaps she has," replied her Grace; "though she has no business to leave before I do."

However, the fact of her niece having gone home did not trouble her much, so she began to quiz the people and cut-up their characters and dresses for the amusement of her friend Lady Mountchessington.

After the play was over, a hired carriage, with some large boxes on it, might have been seen standing in Half Moon Street. Two figures came out of a brilliantly-illuminated house in Curzon Street, and stepped into it.

"Charing Cross!" is the order given to the driver, and off they go.

The two insides feel very happy. They

are launched on the sea of life together, with no rudder or compass to guide their barque but each other's love. They are like two mariners turned adrift on the pathless ocean, but, unlike them, they have no fears or terrors for the future: the present is *all in all*, the past is all forgotten, and love enshrouds the future with a rose-coloured halo.

Of course, "respectable" people will say they were very naughty and very wicked, but then they were very happy; besides, does Whitey Brown make marriages, or are they made in heaven?

Two got into the twelve o'clock mail train for the Continent that night; they looked very like Paris and la belle Hélène. Perhaps it *was* them!

CHAPTER V.

MR. SMALL'S PRYINGS.

"The most sure method of subjecting yourself to be deceived, is to consider yourself more cunning than others."
La Rochefoucauld.

R. SMALL was sitting in his uncomfortable windsor chair, reading a letter, whilst another lay unopened beside him.

It will be remembered that he posted two letters before he went to Wilderness Alley, on the day he saw Lady George Fitzreine come out of it, and scaled the lamp-post to look in at the upper window of an Englishman's castle, viz., his second-floor front.

The letter he was reading was from Inspector Roberts, head constable of Fenacre. It ran thus:—

"SIR,—I am in receipt of yours. The prisoner [Roberts always called a *suspect* a prisoner] is one of the most desperate characters in the town: he has been repeatedly convicted before the Bench at Fenacre, and committed, for terms varying from three months to two years, to the county gaol. This has not improved his general conduct—in fact, he comes out each time with an increased contempt for the laws of his country, and a more settled resolve to break them again on the first opportunity. He owns a lighter, which plies between here and the port of London, and is now absent on one of his nefarious errands. He has taken an idiot, whom the people call 'Daft John,' with him, though *why* he has done so is a mystery. The most probable solution of it is, that he is afraid of his *blabbing* during his absence, as he is next to no use on board.

"I am, Sir,
 Your obedient Servant,
  "ROBERTS, *Head Constable.*"

Mr. Roberts always signed himself simply by his patronymic, like a peer of the realm: he fancied it gave increased weight and dignity to his epistles.

Mr. Small sat and mused a little while, but he was not a man who was long putting "two and two" together, so he exclaimed, after a few moments' reflection, "*I've seen that man!*" Then he took up his other letter, and broke the seal: it was from his *employé* at Pluto's—the unscrupulous servant who sold his master's secrets for base £ s. d., and a very traitor in the camp!

The following is a translation of the original document, which was written in cipher:—

"In answer to yours, the party you name has frequented here, but has not been here lately—was last seen near the river."

This letter was not signed, in case it fell into other hands than those for whom it was intended. Cunning begets cunning, and people who are continually watching and exercising *espionage* on their neighbours and the public in general, become a kind of miniature Machiavellis in all they think and do.

The satellites of St. Martin-le-Grand would not have been much the wiser if they *had* read Mr. Small's communication, but it was safer to make that contingency an *impossibility*. His motto was the word "caution," and he wrapped himself on all occasions in a shroud of impenetrability.

When he had read both the letters carefully over a second time, he locked them up in his desk with a heap of others, all neatly docketed and speared. Then he sat down again, and began to lay his plans. Like a skilful architect, he built his superstructure on a solid foundation: he never attempted anything till he had a firm basis for his operations. His first thought was his "case" Charles Forrester; here was not much difficulty; he was singing every night at "Her Highness's;" and once he made inquiries, he could soon discover his place of residence, and communicate it to Lady Fenacre—his task would then be done. If he had known the gallic language, he would have called it a *fait accompli*; but he did not, so he fell into the vulgarism of terming it "settling his 'ash." Mr. Small was guileless of the letter H as when he came into this wicked world, fifty years ago, and a few odd months added thereunto. But his grand dilemma was the violent end of Sir Richard Fenacre. It fairly puzzled him, and he felt, as he would have termed it, completely " nonplused!" According to all precedents, it could be no one but Rube Rue; but then those letters on the bullet—it *was* a mystery.

The result of his deliberations was that he would run down to Fenacre. You could always pick up more on the scene of action than by hearsay forty miles off. Mr. Small was a man who, when he had decided to do a thing, immediately *did* it. Procrastination was not one of his besetting sins. He had read how fatal to grand enterprises a wavering spirit had been, and he had forthwith determined henceforth to be " firm, sharp, and decisive." In three minutes he was in a hansom, *en route* to Fenacre.

We have witnessed the Grange under

the worst circumstances, during the fogs of winter. It now presented its best aspect, it being the height of summer.

The dreary waste was transformed into great plains of grass, dotted over by innumerable herds of cattle, who were feeding on its luxuriant pasture. The grass was *intensely* green, much of the colour of pickles boiled in copper.

This last was Mr. Small's simile as he walked up from the station.

Mr. Small walked in a leisurely way on the grass by the side of the raised causeway, no longer necessary for the use of pedestrians. He rang the bell at the postern door of the east tower, and stood awaiting an answer on the stone steps.

They were the same steps Sir Richard had descended when he went for his last row.

"It's a queer old place!" remarked Mr.

Small to himself, "and did ought to have a ghost attached."

The door was opened by Mr. Webster, who looked as fat and rubicund as of yore.

"Can I see the place?" asked Mr. Small.

"Certainly, sir," he replied. "Most happy to show it you."

He scented a half crown, did the chief butler.

"It's a curious old place, and was visited by her Majesty Queen Elizabeth of pious memory when she reviewed the soldiers preparatory to their sinking the 'vincible Armada. Here you see her portrait in the style of the period when ruffs was worn high in the neck. Here is the portrait of the Fenacre who was Baronet at that time, and here is his lady dressed just like her blessed Majesty of pious memory. Here is the sword used by him to kill thirty Spaniards aboard the admiral's ship; dulce moriamur patria est," wound up the butler, who was getting breathless.

"You've had sad misfortunes here lately," remarked Mr. Small.

"Ay! that we have! Poor Sir Richard: he was a gen'l'man: took his port till the last! His brother ain't fit to 'old a candle to him: drinks nothing but your wishy-washy French 'bojolly,' as he calls it, as is enough to set the hinside on hedge!"

Then Mr. Webster shivered in a manner indicative of his contempt for all clarets and light wines, and his evidently disagreeable reminiscences of their taste and flavour.

Then the butler led Mr. Small up a winding staircase to the roof of the east tower.

"From this here eminence," quoth he,

"you can see the 'hole township of Fenacre, together with the hextensive range of marshes; halso the sea, over which on very clear days you see the white cliffs of sunny France."

Mr. Webster had learnt all this from the Essex Guide Book, which noticed Fenacre Grange as a "curious old Elizabethan building, celebrated as being the residence of Queen Elizabeth during the muster of the troops on the marshes to repel the attack of the Spaniards, who were expected to land from their fleet, which they vaingloriously termed the *Invincible* Armada."

However, luckily for Mr. Webster, a mighty wind blew the fleet up to the Orkneys, as he was enabled to wind up with the moral truism:

"But Providence frustrated their knavish tricks, and here we all are, safe and sound. God save the Queen!"

There was a flag-staff on the tower, and Mr. Small, who was of a practical turn of mind, asked what was the use of it.

"Use!" exclaimed the butler, "why we runs up a flag when the fam'ly's down, to hinform the *canal* of that fact. It is done at Windsor Castle, I am told," continued he, pompously, "and the Fenacres have been loyal to the backbone, sir, ever since this time of her blessed majesty Queen Elizabeth, of pious mem'ry, who when the invin——"

"I honour them for it!" said Mr. Small, with warmth. "I honour them for it!"

He was afraid of having the whole story of the Armada trotted out again for his especial gratification.

What a bore it is when Smith, at a dinner party, begins his old story about "When I was at Calcutta, you know it was awfully hot, and the punkah-wallah went to sleep;

and Chutnee of 'ours,' who was infernally peppery, threw a knife at him," &c., &c. Who has not *groaned* when Smith, for the 555th night, as the playbill says, commences "When I was at Cal——"? It ought to be a recognised law of society that any one who has heard it before should be exempt from the trouble of grinning when it commences, and should be allowed to sip his or her port, as the case may be, in solemn silence, and stoical indifference to Chutnee's infernally peppery temper!

Under the roof of the east tower was a small chamber which Webster pompously termed the armoury. It answered to the room known as the "gun-room" in country-houses. Besides the modern breech-loaders and long "wild-duck" shooters, it contained a few old yeomanry swords, an arquebuss, and one or two rusty helmets and old pieces of armour.

On a table under the window was a quantity of shot-belts, powder-flasks, ramrods, bullet-moulds, *et id genus omne*. Mr. Small began to turn them over and examine them.

"This helmet," said Mr. Webster, "was worn by Sir Henry Fenacre, *temp.* Queen Elizabeth of pious mem'ry, during the repulse of the invin——"

"Bother the Armada!" said the irreverent Mr. Small, with impatience.

"What did you say, sir?" said the butler, with a searching glance.

"I said drat the Armada, and Queen Elizabeth too," he replied.

"We had better go down, I think," said the butler.

He did not *say* any more than this, but he looked *unutterable* things. What a pass the world was coming to, when men went about dratting Queen Elizabeth and the

"Invincible" Armada! The world was waxing evil with a vengeance, if those were sentiments openly vouched. Perhaps it was some hired spy in the pay of France or America! He determined, come what might, to strike a blow for his country, though he might perish in the fight.

"It's a bulwark of the constitution, a glory of all lands, a sweet-smelling savour, a very foundation stone of all our national stability, a blow to the Papacy, which has caused it to rock in its shoes ever since."

"What's made it rock?" asked Mr. Small.

"Her blessed Majesty Queen Elizabeth, of pious mem'ry, and the *so-called* 'INVINCIBLE' Armada!"

"Drat 'em!" said Mr. Small.

The chief butler looked on him with contempt too withering for words.

Mr. Webster had employed his leisure hours in reading; but what he read did not *arrange* itself in his head. The Psalms, the History of England, and a treatise on the best method of cleaning plate, were all jumbled up together in his ideas.

"What's the best inn in the town?" Mr. Small asked, as he left the Grange, and slipped five shillings into the butler's hand.

"The Dagenham Arms possesses 'good accommodation for man and beast,'" he replied, quoting verbatim from the sign-board.

"I don't care about the beasts," said Mr. Small, "not happening to be one; but if they know how to make a *man* comfortable, I'll go there."

"You'll get the very best of everything, I assure you," said Mr. Webster; "the very best. Good morning, sir."

Then Mr. Small strolled leisurely over the marshes to the town, and went to the police-station. He found Roberts, the presiding *genius loci*, busily engaged in copying reports. He rose and greeted his London *confrère* with great cordiality, and invited him into his sanctum to discuss the merits of a round of cold beef. Of course the conversation turned on professional business. Talking " shop" is not confined to one class of society: it pervades all.

Parsons talk " shop" when they meet: ritualism, schools, vestments, and old women. City men hobnob together over " Turks," " Moscow gas," " Bundlecund preference shares," and " Monte Video debentures." Lawyers treat of leases, disputed will-cases, points of law, rights of way, and six-and-eightpence. Military men get animated over the " Queen's Regulations" and pipeclay. Naval, over three-deckers or ironclads, monitors, and the wind's eye, and so on, *ad infinitum*. Therefore, seeing there is clerical " shop," City ditto, also military, naval, theatrical, literary, &c., why should not there be *police* " shop?" There *is;* and you will see it from the conversation of Small and Roberts.

"I have been over the Grange this morning. It's a rum old place, and there is a rum old cove in charge: talks of nothing but Queen Elizabeth and the Spanish Armada."

"I know him," replied Roberts. "It's a way he's got into from showing off the place."

"Then the sooner he gets out of the place the better," said Mr. Small. "I nearly punched his head for him."

"Nothing stirring about the murder?" asked Roberts.

"Well," said Mr. Small, "I should like to see that bullet as did the deed."

"Why?"

"Because I should like to see if it was

cast in this," replied Mr. Small, throwing a bullet-mould on the table.

"Whew!" whistled Roberts, taking it up and examining it. "It's got some letters scratched inside it."

"That's why I took it," said Small.

"*How* did you get it?"

"Why, when that old fool was ranting about Queen Elizabeth and the Armada, I turned over the things on the table, and slipped this into my pocket."

Then they both leant back in their chairs and laughed heartily. It was a stroke of cunning they could both appreciate thoroughly. It was a "shoppy" kind of joke, and they enjoyed it amazingly.

"Ha! ha! ha!" they laughed, like a chorus of stage-peasants.

"Have you any idea *where* the bullet is?" asked Mr. Small, when he *could* speak.

"Old Webster told me Sir John locked

it up in his drawer when Dr. Spires gave it him. He knows it's true what he says, because he told me he was looking through the keyhole all the time, and saw and heard everything."

"He ought to be one of us," said Mr. Small.

"He hasn't got the discretion requisite," replied Roberts. "He ain't one of those fellows who can *worm* things out, and tell nothing in return. He's too fond of talking for *our* profession."

"So I should think, from my experience of him this morning." Then Mr. Small burst out laughing, as he thought of Queen Elizabeth and the Spanish Armada.

"The letters are 'L. F.,'" said Roberts, taking up the bullet-mould.

"What do they stand for?" asked Mr. Small.

"Loftus Fenacre," he replied. "There's a nephew of Sir John of that name."

"I know: I met him at the Duchess of Maldon's 'At home,'" said Mr. Small, with dignity, "and he was carrying-on uncommon with his cousin, the present Baronet's daughter—a handsome gal, with yellow hair, and great black eyes."

The unsophisticated rustic, Inspector Roberts, thought Mr. Small had been an invited guest of her Grace's; and that the profession was getting that recognition in the fashionable world that its importance entitled it to, at last.

"I should like to be in London myself," he said, with a sigh. "There's such a field for talent there. I am literally wasted down here amongst lighters and barges."

"It's not so wearing, a country life," said Mr. Small.

"I'd rather *wear* out than *rust* out," replied Roberts.

In his whitewashed room at Fenacre,

he often longed for the glories of the great metropolis.

"I shall go up to the Grange again," said Mr. Small, "and say I left my umbrella."

"Very good. The bullet's in the left-hand top drawer of the bureau. Old Webster said it was."

"I think I've seen Rube Rue," said Mr. Small. "A large heavy man: he's got an idiot with him,—at least, should say so from the voice."

"That's him!" said Roberts, excitedly. "Up to no good, wherever he is, I warrant. Directly he sets foot in the place, I arrest him on a charge of highway robbery on the London road. He'll get seven years if I can get it for him, by swearing black's white, even!"

"That's right," said Mr. Small. "The criminal classes should be waged war against, root and branch!"

"I wish I could collect some evidence against him, so as to have him tried for Sir Richard's murder: his character is so bad that any jury would give a verdict of 'guilty' against him without caring whether the witnesses were for or against."

"Couldn't that idiot be made to peach?" asked Mr. Small.

"No go!" replied Roberts. "He's a case of *non compos*; don't know his head from his heels."

"Not if he was coached up what to say?"

"Well, it's just *possible*, but it is as likely as not he'd forget it clean when he got into court."

"When you get Rube for this robbery, we'll bring the affair on the *tappys*, I'd like to see it cleared up."

"So should I."

"I must go to the Grange at once, or I shall miss the last up-train. Good night."

It was getting dusk as Mr. Small walked across the marshes to the Grange. The bells round the necks of the cattle were tinkling melodiously in the distance, and the whole scene presented an appearance of pastoral tranquillity. There was a light burning in the study. Mr. Webster was sitting there reading the *Essex Calf*. Mr. Small concealed his umbrella at the bottom of the stone steps, and walked up boldly and rang the bell.

The door was opened by Webster.

"I have left my umbrella here," said Mr. Small. "I think up in the armoury. I was so engrossed by your interesting narrative of the Armada, that I entirely forgot it."

"I'll go up and get it," replied the butler, who was willing to oblige a man who had just given him five shillings by so trifling a service. "Will you wait in here?" Then he showed him into the study, where there was a light burning.

Mr. Small listened carefully as Webster ascended the staircase; then he locked the door, and took a leisurely survey of the room. There was a heavy bureau on one side, with drawers on each side, and a hole in the middle for the writer's legs.

"In the left-hand top drawer," he said to himself. Then he pulled out a small bunch of skeleton keys and opened it. The first thing that met his eyes was *the* bullet. He caught it up hastily and relocked the drawer. Then he opened the door and listened: he could hear Webster come panting down from the armoury.

"It ain't there," he said, when he got to the bottom.

"It is not of the slightest consequence," replied Mr. Small. "I must have left it somewhere else. I wont trouble you any further, and will say good night, as I have to catch the train for London."

When the door closed, Mr. Small picked up his umbrella, and went gaily over the waste. It was true he had just told a lie, but he did not feel any moral degradation on account of it. He told more in one day than there were hairs on his head—it was his profession. And yet he felt no remorse. A "good" lie that bore fruit was to him as the brilliant achievement of Waterloo was to Wellington—an epoch to be looked back upon with pride.

There is nothing more contemptible than a liar. Truth is the brightest gem in the diadem of honour, and the most precious jewel of chivalry! but all this is too high-flown for proprietors of private inquiry offices, like Mr. Small; they do not understand it, nor can they appreciate its worth, which is "far above rubies," let alone diamonds of the first water.

When Mr. Small got into the train at Fenacre, he pulled out his private key and locked himself in the carriage; he wanted to examine the bullet narrowly.

It is useful to have a railway key; people seldom take the trouble to get your carriage opened by the railway official; they get contentedly into the next.

Mr. Small sat immediately under the lamp: it was a hot night, and the windows were open; and he could see the lights in the rigging of the ships on the Thames. He first pulled the bullet-mould carefully out of his pocket, and after a long survey placed it carefully on the seat opposite to him. Then he took out the bullet. Very faint, yet very distinct were the letters "L. F." He compared them with the marks in the mould: they coincided exactly! it could have been cast in no other. What was he to think then? Rube Rue could never have had access to the Fenacre armoury; it must have been some one in the house. The fact was indisputable.

"He and his nephew weren't on terms," thought Mr. Small. "My suspicions are roused!—*it is Loftus Fenacre*, as I'm a living man! and I'll prove it. I'll bring it home to him, step by step. He shall die on the scaffold, and I'll add 1000*l.* to my account at Dock's."

CHAPTER VI.

ON BOULOGNE PIER.

"They say, best men are moulded out of faults;
And for the most, become much more the better
For being a little bad."—SHAKSPEARE.

ORD HENRY FITZREINE was pacing up and down the pier at Boulogne, smoking a cigar, and feeling very dismal over his compulsory expatriation. "What a fool I've been!" he said to himself; "but I am glad I didn't do the *post obit*." He was watching amongst other of his countrymen, the Folkestone packet swiftly making its way over the green waters, and leaving a white track of foam in its wake.

It is the one amusement of the British, who by cruel fate are compelled to reside "over the sea,"—like a certain Charlie, famous in Jacobite song, did of yore—to go down to the pier and see the boat from England come in. The ball at the flag-staff was up, as a signal that the water would not admit of the entrance of the steamer into the harbour till the tide rose.

It was a dreadful thing for the novices on Neptune's domain not being able to land at once, but having to remain rolling and tossing about in the open sea in sight of land.

However, they may be sure they will get no pity from their countrymen, who are enjoying their distress from the vantage ground of the pier. "They'll *all* be down," they say, with a chuckle, "every man Jack of them!" Then they give vent to their joy at each roll and pitch of the packet, and gloat over the agonies of the *voyageurs*. At length the ball drops, and the paddle-wheels begin to turn slowly, and she steams up to the side of the quay. All the British make a rush to the side of the pier to see them land.

"How miserable that chap looks!" they say; then they all laugh heartily.

Is misery in *any* form a subject of mirth and amusement? It would seem it is from the uncontrollable laughter of our respected countrymen on Boulogne and other piers at the sight of "poor humanity," who has been offering a propitiatory sacrifice to the little fishes.

Queen joined in the laugh with the others, though he himself was very wretched at heart; he'd only got a pound left in his pocket, and he did not, as "worldlings" say, "know what the deuce to do" to add another thereunto.

However, the present is everything, and

he laughed heartily at poor humanity who had been very ill on the " waste of waters."

There arose a babel of shouts from the fishwomen who carry the luggage, the drivers of the *voitures de place*, the touts from the different hotels, the itinerant sellers of fruit, the vendors of *bière à l'Anglaise*, &c., the burden of which was that their commodities were the best, and that they themselves were the most honest, most trustworthy, and most self-laudatory individuals in the whole Pas-de-Calais, let alone the town of Boulogne.

Queen scanned all the people narrowly as they came up the ladder, but he was fearful of Philistines in pursuit, so he kept himself prudently in the background.

The steamer contained the usual passengers, who fly to the Continent at the end of the season, to recruit their jaded energies amongst the vineyard-clad banks of the Rhine, or the eternal snows of the Alps. There were Belgravian mothers with flocks of daughters who had not "gone off" during the season, and whom they hoped to hook husbands for at the Swiss *table d'hôtes.* They were, one and all, *so* charmed with the freshness of all they saw abroad ; it was so *very* different to England. There were young men from Oxford and Cambridge, who were going to do the grand tour before the stern voice of "Alma Mater" recalled them to their studies at the Universities; and "young" ladies of a certain age, who had come abroad with the hopes of attracting attention by their originality and strong-mindedness. *They* were above the folly of dressing in the style of the period. "Give me a good plain gingham," they said, "that wont tear on the mountains." They meant to do everything, and see everything, from Kursaals to

Popish practices. Then there were the travellers, or agents I believe they call themselves, who were carrying samples of hardware and cutlery for their employers, and tried to look as if they were not, but were only travelling for pleasure. These men wear the "complete tourist's suit at thirty-six, warranted quite the thing for foreign travel," and are, with a few exceptions, most insufferable specimens of the genus "snob" who wander about the world.

We have a "Galloping Snob," why should not his exploits be celebrated higher than those of the itinerant Jew? By Jove! I'll write a book some day, and call it the "Wandering Snob." I will depict him in steam-packets, railway carriages, and omnibuses. I will represent him at *table d'hôtes*, talking about his "place" in Essex. I will paint him with his hat on in church, where he is grinning at the " Popish mummeries," as he calls them; writing his name, John Jones, on the Pyramids, and under the left eye of the Sphynx; in the court-yard of the Invalides, laughing at the cripples; in the Colosseum at Rome, remarking that Julius Cæsar was a horrid old fool; on the Righi, saying Primrose Hill beats it to fits; in Seville Cathedral, winking at the nuns behind the grating; in the Rue St. Honoré, saying, "Mild-End Road is infinitely superior;" in the Forest of Fontainebleau, saying Epping is the best; at Waterloo, chipping off pieces of granite from the monument, and inscribing his name thereon; swaggering in the Broadway at New York; cursing the "black beasts" in Calcutta; at Longwood hacking up the willow-tree with his pocket-knife; at Thebes carrying off pieces of mummy—in fact, all over the world, where the "Wandering Snob" has made himself famous by his vulgarity.

Queen saw all these specimens of the *genus homo* come up the ladder, and " many more besides;" at length he started, and gave way to his favourite ejaculation, namely, an appeal to the king of the gods —Jove.

" By Jove !" said Queen, " who'd have thought of this !"

Very slowly, and looking very wan and pale, his cousin, Minnie Snowdrop, was ascending the ladder.

" I suppose the old woman is with her," said Queen to himself, " coming to look after me?"

By the " old woman" Queen meant her Grace the Duchess of Maldon, his mother, whose maternal solicitude he conjectured might have led her to cross the Channel in search of her prodigal son.

But his wisdom was at fault here; for, instead of an old woman, up came a very young man. It was only six months ago that he was at Eton, and did not mind being called a boy, but now he was hurt by it: he felt it derogatory to his dignity as an officer in her Majesty's service.

Herein is a notable difference between the two sexes: the noble sex, *i.e.*, the male, are always very anxious to drop the name of *boy;* the other hang on to the title of *girl* long after they have passed maturity. I know of "girls" who are forty if they are a day; they are loth to give up the name even when grey hairs begin to crop up, and there is a notable falling off in the thickness and quantity of the back hair; they cling to the name like grim death.

"This is a rum go!" said Queen. "I'll watch and see what takes place."

They were both standing on the stone

quay, collecting their boxes in a little heap round them, as the porters carried them up from the deck of the steamer.

Minnie was dressed in a dark blue serge, and a yachting hat. I don't know that she felt altogether at ease: she felt she had been doing " those things which she ought not to have done," and was rather vague in her ideas as to the consequences of the step she had taken. However, these thoughts do not weigh much upon " sweet seventeen," who is, or fancies herself to be, very much devoted to the little naked god Cupid. So when she began to get, what sailors call " land legs," she threw all those doubts to the four winds, and abandoned herself to the pleasure of the hour. There had been a dash of novelty and independence about the whole affair, which in itself is a source of gratification to those whom the wheels of Time's chariot have not passed over very often; besides, was not it very pleasant to be loved? not with any mediocre devotion, or divided affection, but with the passion of a soul.

Victor Hugo, in " Les Misérables," makes Marcus write to Cosette, " God can add nothing to the happiness of those who love, except giving them endless duration. After a life of love, an eternity of love is in truth an augmentation; but it is impossible, even for God, to increase in its intensity the ineffable felicity which love gives to the soul in this world. God is the fulness of heaven, love is the fulness of man." " When love has blended and moulded two beings in an angelic and sacred union, they have found the secret of life; henceforth they are only the two terms of the same destiny, the two wings of one mind." So wrote Marcus Pontmercy to his well-beloved.

If any one supposes that the people who

figure in the "meat" of the "sandwich" of the first column in the *Times* have these sentiments, they are vastly mistaken. For the most part with them it is: "So much per annum, a carriage, so many opera boxes, a certain number of stall-tickets, three weeks at the seaside, ten days at Brighton in November, and a jointure at the decease of the husband, or a life interest in the wife's capital, if she should happen to die first!"

This represents love in the nineteenth century: it is bought and sold like railway shares or debentures. A man with a good balance at his banker's, buys love as he would paintings or statues. A woman who has got any beauty to boast of, sells it, as a rule, to the highest bidder, condescends to spend her husband's money, and shelters her indiscretions behind the shield of his name. Love has become a courtesan, and says, " Give me so much, and I will give you love." There is hardly to be found such a thing as *disinterested* love: it went out with our great-grandmothers, wooden hoops, hearts, and other old fashioned follies, which would be anachronisms in the present days, as much out of place as the "myths of the Middle Ages" in this century of science and civilization.

I said Minnie abandoned herself to the pleasure of being loved; not for anything she had belonging to her; not for Three-per-Cents. and Bank securities; but for *herself*, and that alone.

First love is the most intense in its devotion, because of its *newness*. Do not we enjoy novelty more than anything we have been satiated with? In the nursery did not we like bread-and-jam with an overweening fondness, simply because we did not have it every day? It is the same with love; the *first* is the one that engrosses our very beings; after that we get used to it, and look on it in a very commonplace way, and think no more of being in love than going in to dinner. When Byron wrote his stanzas on Antony and Cleopatra, he expressed a wish that the hero and heroine were in their *première jeunesse*, instead of being somewhat advanced in years, because he liked celebrating youthful passion in his verses, not that of maturity. He probably held this theory himself, *vide* his continual reference to Miss Chaworth in his letters; besides, of course Antony and Cleopatra had had dozens of "affairs" before they came across each other, and their amours had not the charm of novelty or the zest of newness. The proverb says, "There's no fool like an old fool." Now to apply this; spoony *young* people make great fools of themselves when under the dominion of Cupid, but *old* people are ten thousand times worse. It produces a feeling of *nausea* to see them indulge in physical demonstrations of affection; to see a damsel of fifty go up in playful manner and throw her fat or withered arm round the bald pate of her *fiancé* of sixty, who is afflicted with the gout at times, and is chronically bilious! It is a perfectly galling and nauseating sight! So much for "old fools" in love: now for the young ones.

Is is *just* bearable to witness a similar pantomime between two very young people under the influence of *la grande passion*, but even *they* should keep such ebullitions of feeling for private performance, and not afford the public gratuitous amusement at their expense. I should be afraid to say what fools Charlie and Minnie had made of themselves *en route* to Boulogne; how they had sat holding each other's hands, and committed other follies peculiar to people in love; how they thought eternity could not be long enough for their happiness, and that a severed life would be worse than death to them. How they wished they were the Siamese twins, which would put separation entirely and utterly out of the question at once. These and other kindred follies had occupied them since they had left London, on the night of Lady George's theatricals. When they had collected their little colony of boxes, they got into a *fiacre* and drove to the station of the Chemin de fer du Nord, and went on by the first train to Paris, whither at some future time we will follow them, and see whether "Love in a Cottage" is really as delightful in the realization as in the anticipation.

Meanwhile Queen had kept prudently in the background: he did not wish to be seen or recognised by his cousin. "It's the rummiest go I ever saw," he said. " Beats cockfighting hollow!" Then he went back to the Hôtel de l'Europe, in the rue de l'Ecu, where he was "hanging out," and took pen and paper, and sat down to write a letter.

Writing a letter was with Queen a very serious affair, and not to be "enterprised or taken in hand unadvisedly;" it was an affair of weighty deliberation and profound thought.

The epistle was inscribed to his mother, "The Duchess of Maldon, Maldon Lodge, Inverness, N.B." Queen knew that the family were going up to Scotland, where the Duke had a shooting-box, as soon as the season was over. When he had directed the envelope in his best text-hand, he did not know how on earth to go on with the contents which it was destined to convey. "My dear Mother," he wrote; then he altered it to "Dear Mother," without the "My." "I have always been told that in a business letter," said he, " you should put as few words as possible. George used to say that's what they did at the ' Red Tape.' " Then he took up his pen again and wrote, " I am in a deuce of a mess "—then he scratched that out, thinking it would not do. Then he put, " owing to involved circumstances" —that'll do splendidly; it sounds business-like!—" I have been obliged to leave London unexpectedly for the Continent. I had not time to bring any money with me, and should be obliged if you would forward me a cheque, as my own account at Dock's is overdrawn.

" I remain your affectionate son,

" Henry Fitzreine.
" Hôtel de l'Europe, Boulogne."

He read and re-read his production, over and over again; then he put it in the envelope, and took up his hat, and went to the

Post-office, in the Grand Rue; then he went to a jeweller's shop, and bought the most showy French gold necklace and bracelets that the establishment contained; then he went home and did it up in a parcel ready to send to England. When he had accomplished all this he felt quite pleased with himself, and ordered luncheon forthwith.

Amongst the crowd of English who witnessed the arrival of the Folkestone packet was a middle-aged lady, very quietly dressed in black, and a young man of about four-and-twenty, apparently her son. They occupied handsome apartments in the Rue de Tivoli, and were seemingly well-endowed with the loaves and fishes of this life. At least, so their compatriots said of them, and it is an unusual thing amongst the foreigners residing at Boulogne-sur-mer; they are all more or less "out at elbows," or if they have a balance at their banker's, have no character to speak of.

The lady was a widow; at least, she said she was. Her name was Raynor; her son was called Alured Raynor, and they kept themselves to themselves. The residents had called upon them, but had one and all met with a stern and uncompromising "not at home." After the lapse of a fortnight their visits were returned by a deep black-edged envelope, containing two cards with equally broad borders, on which were printed the words, "Mrs. Raynor," "Mr. Alured Raynor." At first, people bowed to them when they met on the pier in the morning, but at length they had given them up; it was no use bowing to people and never getting any further, so they gave them up. They gave no dinners, *soirées*, or "*thé-dansantes*, and "worldlings" do not care to know people whom they cannot get anything out of. It is an unnecessary trouble altogether. "Worldlings" seldom or never take any trouble about anybody whom it is not an advantage to them in some way to know. Mr. Alured Raynor passed his time in study; he was going to Heidelberg University, and was ambitious of academical honours.

This was all the *quidnuncs* of Boulogne had been able to glean about the Raynors, and this had been extorted from his tutor, a broken-down senior wrangler from Cambridge, in a confidential after-supper *tête-à-tête* with Mrs. Colonel Chutnee, who was rather the Queen of British Boulogne. At least, she was lady patroness at all the balls, and had a stall at all the charity bazaars, and was secretary to the Society for the Relief of Shipwrecked Mariners, and president of the Ladies' Amalgamated Flannel Petticoat Society: the English part of the Boulognese, like the Athenians of old, have nothing else to do but to hear and tell some new thing. Mrs. Colonel Chutnee was the very princess of gossips. By eleven A.M. she knew whether her friends had got soup or fish for dinner that night; after a ball she knew what "he said," and "she said," on each occasion, and had spoilt more than one eligible match by her tattling propensities.

She did not live with her husband, Colonel Chutnee, late of the Bengal Tigers, whom we have seen in Sir Alfred's waiting-room. There *was* a story going the round of Boulogne about a certain Doctor out in India, when she was up at Simla. But she had steadily lived it down, and by going to church on saints' days, and becoming president of the "Amalgamated Ladies," she had established her respectability on a firm basis. Whatever it was, the residents forgave her sins, if the Colonel did not, and she was the acknowledged leader of *ton* in British Boulogne.

After her *tête-à-tête* with the wrangler, she said to the English, "*I* shall call on the Raynors." Then they all went and did the same. If Mrs. Colonel Chutnee did, why it was undoubtedly "the" thing to do; so they did it. With what result has been already shown.

"I don't believe the woman's a widow at all," said Mrs. Colonel Chutnee over her tea. Considering the Doctor, she might have held her tongue.

All the people had taken their cue from her, and when they had been two months in the town, every one had ceased to bow to them or think anything more about them.

Alured Raynor was a slightly-built man, with black hair and black eyes; he wore a settled look of deep melancholy dejection; he was never seen to smile. "He's got something on his conscience," said Mrs. Colonel Chutnee. Considering how lightly the Doctor sat upon her, this was a marvel to her. "Let bygones be bygones," was her motto.

She kept this rule intact as far as she was concerned personally, but her acquaintances experienced no such clemency at her hands; on the contrary, she kept a correct catalogue of their sins and shortcomings from the remotest time up to the present moment.

The Raynors' apartments in the Rue de Tivoli were extremely comfortable, and handsomely furnished, and the mother and son were sitting at luncheon together after their morning walk on to the pier.

"When does Layman think you will be ready for Heidelberg?"

"In about two months," replied her son; "that is, if I work very hard. I shall be obliged to have a private tutor whilst at the college. You can't learn in a month or two what you ought to have been acquiring bit by bit all your life!"

"True," said Mrs. Raynor, with a sigh, "you labour under great disadvantages; but my unfortunate circumstances rendered it impossible for me to give you any better education than you have had."

"I don't reproach you, mother, but that man. He did you and me a cruel wrong."

"Hush! You have had your revenge, remember. I loved him very dearly once."

"And I hated him, and hate him now! But I had my revenge," he continued, triumphantly. "I had my revenge!"

"Don't speak in that way," said Mrs. Raynor; "for pity's sake, don't recall any circumstances of that wretched night. You'll make me hate you if you do!"

" Alured's look of triumph was gone; it

was only on his face for a moment; it had given place to gnawings now of remorse.

"I wont mention it," he said; "you are the only being that ever loved me, and I will not say anything to make you weep." Then he shuddered, and said, "Oh! that wretched night!" in a despairing tone. "Do you believe in the 'possession' of the devil?" asked Alured; "because he was in me that night; it was not I, but he that did it. I would give worlds to recall the past, but," he continued, in a low voice, "I had my revenge, and it was very sweet at first; but oh! it has left a bitter taste behind it—a taste that will cloy all pleasure that it may be my lot to enjoy, when it comes to me. I shall eat and find it bitter, like the apples of the Dead Sea. One phantom will for ever haunt me—remorse! Yet I have had *revenge!*" he continued—"my *revenge!*"

Then he rose up slowly and went to his books, which were piled up on an escritoire in the back room, and was soon absorbed in study. He sat at his books till it grew dark, and the lamps began to twinkle in the streets. He felt sad and weary: *it* was always with him, that phantom, "remorse!"

Queen had none of these feelings, and danced gaily at the *établissement* with the *grisettes*, who were much amused at his pronunciation of the French language. All the English knowing that he was a "Lord" bowed down to him at once. Mrs. Colonel Chutnee introduced herself to him, and offered him the *entrée* of good society. Queen began to think expatriation was very jolly after all, and that the white cliffs of Old England were all sentimental twaddle.

But when he went down to the pier the next morning, after having "done" the column and all the lions, he felt heartily sick of it. "It's all the same thing," he said. Not even the sprightly conversation of Mrs. Colonel Chutnee was able to atone for the tameness of everything around; not but that the waves and sands were sparkling in the sunshine, and all nature looked particularly bright and cheerful; but *he* did not feel so. If one *is* dull, by all means let us have dull weather; it is more suitable. If I have *les diables bleus*, give me a wet, foggy day to enjoy them, not a day all light and sunshine, that makes them look bluer than ever by force of contrast; let everything match exactly in the atmosphere our frames and feelings, else we feel inclined to vituperate the weather, and stigmatize it as confoundedly perverse.

CHAPTER VII.

MADELEINE REFUSES A DUKE'S ELDEST SON.

"Soft as the memory of buried love,
Pure as the prayer which childhood wafts above,
Was she."—BYRON.

MALDON LODGE, N.B., is a Gothic erection of white stone, with a blue slate roof. It stands in the middle of a belt of fir-trees, which stretch out like wings on each side of it. There is a grassplat in front, with a carriage-drive round; beyond this there is a low stone balustrade and then a ditch, by courtesy termed a moat. This separates the home-fields from the moor, which stretches like a sea of barrenness all round the fertile little island. The Lodge was built by his Grace's father, the late Duke of Maldon, and is by no means to be compared with his ancestral seat in Essex, Maldon Castle, which is situated in the south part of that county, amidst a richly-wooded scenery.

The owner of the Lodge was sitting by the open window, with a newspaper in his hand, awaiting the arrival of the rest of the party for breakfast.

" Every one late, as usual. How I *have* been kept waiting!"

This feeling is by no means confined to the Duke of Maldon; it very generally pervades society. There are some people who never *are* ready for anything. If you told them that dinner was to be at 6.30, and by a mental reservation you had settled that the feast should be holden at seven, they would know it by *instinct*, and come in at half-past.

"I'm always down myself," he said. "Why can't other people be?"

Then Madeleine opened the door of the breakfast-room, and came up to him, and held out her hand, and said "Good morning."

The Duke jumped up—he was civil to every one but his wife—and returned her greeting.

"I'm afraid I'm rather late."

"Don't mention it. My wife hasn't been down yet; and wont be for the next half hour, I daresay," he replied.

The fact was that the Duchess was reading Queen's letter, dated from Boulogne, in her dressing-room, and it had rather upset her. She knew the Duke would not give him anything if she asked him to. He had said he would not, and she knew by experience when he once said so, he never altered; and so she would be obliged to do it herself. Henry was her favourite son, but, all the same, it was no joke keeping him going out of her pin-money. Reading and re-reading his letter, she could see but one alternative—to send him money ; and she resolved to write him a cheque and a " blue" after breakfast.

This was what kept her upstairs some time after the appointed hour for breakfast. Meanwhile, all the party in the house had assembled in the breakfast-room, Lady George, Sir John, Madeleine, and Dagenham.

" We wont wait a moment longer," said the Duke; then he pulled the bell with a jerk, for the servants to bring in the hot meat, &c. "Take the top of the table, Lily," he said to Lady George. Her ladyship was nothing loth : she knew it would "rile" her mother-in-law to see her sitting in her place when she came down. Since the escapade that wound up Lady George's theatricals, she and the Duchess had not been on speaking terms. "You're at the bottom of it, I'll swear," her Grace had said. "Your systematic bullying and browbeating is at the bottom of it," Lady George replied. "If you had treated her more like a Christian and less like a dog, she would never have done it. You may thank your stars she hasn't demolished your wig and coiffure for you a dozen times. I would have done if I had been in her place." Since this little ebullition of feeling, they had not spoken *to* each other, but had not ceased to talk *at* one another on every occasion.

The door opened and the Duchess of Maldon came in. Lady George pretended not to see her, and went on pouring out the tea. Sir John rose and shook hands with his hostess, who greeted him with the utmost cordiality.

Then she *looked* at Lady George, who went on steadily with the tea.

"Ain't you going to sit down?" asked the Duke.

"When I get my proper place," she replied, in a pointed manner.

"*I* told Lily to sit there. You ought to be down in time. You didn't suppose I was going to wait for you, did you?"

"If I did, I was mistaken," she replied. Then she took a chair by Sir John.

"I'll have coffee, if you please," said the Duchess to the Baronet.

Now coffee always made her Grace ill if she drank it in the morning; but she would not have tea because Lady George must have poured it out.

Who was punished? Herself or Lady George?

Her ladyship watched her drinking coffee

with much gusto. "How ill she will be!" she thought.

Lord Dagenham was sitting on the other side of the table by Madeleine, as we know his health was immensely improved, and this latter fact had urged Mandarin to "quod" Lord Henry. The heir-apparent was entirely different to the rest of his family; he was neither quarrelsome, a fool, or fast—in short, he was *not* a "worldling," and consequently had not many tastes and sympathies in common with the Maldons.

He did not like Lady George, who was too much of a "highflyer" to suit his tastes. He thought his brother Henry an emptyheaded fool; his father bored him; and his mother disgusted him with her unfortunate snappishness, and general peevishness of temper. That the poor woman had provocation we have all seen, but then he, in common with the world, made no allowances for it.

The world never *do* make allowances for the frailties of their neighbours; if any one does so they are suspected of a fellow-feeling, arising not from pity or compassion, but from having in former times done likewise.

Lord Dagenham, in the exalted circle in which he moved, seldom found any one so entirely free from worldliness as Madeleine; seldom or never came across people who were natural and did not fête and cringe to him, on account of his expectations. He had met Madeleine at his father's house in Grosvenor Square, and it was solely on her account that he had come down to Maldon Lodge, N.B.

"Dagenham will propose to Madeleine Fenacre," her Grace had said to the Duke, on the first night of their arrival in Scotland, "and she'll refuse him!"

"Then she's a fool," replied his Grace. "I should like the match. The estates want propping up with a little of the 'ready,' and she'll have a good round sum of her own. You'd better try what you can do."

As we have seen, it was for her Jacob that the Duchess wanted the heiress, *not* for her first-born. However, she dared not breathe this to the Duke; besides, she said to herself, "Sir John's no fool, and knows the world, and wont throw his money away on a spendthrift younger son; and if Henry can't have her, why I would rather Dagenham did. He ought to marry soon, or some of those tuft-hunters will get him in a corner before he knows where he is!"

"She'll have him like a shot, if he asks her," said the Duke; "any girl would sell her soul for a coronet and strawberry leaves!"

"*Most* of them would," replied his wife, "but not *all*—and she's one of them!"

Her Grace was a great discerner of character, and she had seen a good deal of Madeleine during the season, and she had taken a pretty good mental photograph of her character. "She hasn't got a grain of ambition in her whole character," had been her verdict, and we know that the verdict was far from being an incorrect one.

After breakfast, Madeleine went out in the garden, and Dagenham soon followed her; the Duke and Lady George were left alone in the breakfast-room. They were both standing near the window, when the Duke remarked to Lady George, "I'd bet a fiver that girl has gone into the garden on purpose to get a *tête-à-tête*."

"No, she hasn't," said Lady George; "she's perfectly natural in all she does; she does nothing for effect; everything with her is unstudied and impromptu!"

"I never heard one woman say a good word for another before; upon my life, I haven't!"

"I always give *le diable* his due!" replied Lady George. "I don't like the girl, but I must say she is perfectly natural, and hasn't got a scrap of affectation about her!"

"What's to be done about Minnie Snowdrop?" said the Duke. "Your mother wont hear of forgiving her. I tell her it's all her fault: she bullied her into it."

"Write to her yourself," said Lady George.

"I don't know what to say if I do."

"I'll tell you."

"All right, get me some paper then. I shan't say I have written to anybody."

"Now, are you ready?" said Lady George. "My dear Minnie."

"My dear Minnie," wrote the Duke. "I don't know where to send it to, when it *is* written," he said to Lady George.

"I do," she replied. "Hôtel Mirabeau, rue de la Paix."

"*How* do you know?"

"Because I do."

"Well, that's an unanswerable reason, at all events. I expect you know more about the affair than you choose to say?"

"Can I help it, if a girl chooses to fall in love?"

"No, I suppose not," said his Grace. "I suppose not."

Lady George here showed some of the wisdom of the serpent, by answering a question with another.

"Well, about this letter?"

"Say ' I am surprised and grieved at the step you have taken——' "

The Duke looked up at Lady George

when she said this, with an air of amazement. It was but yesterday that she had fought the battle of the runaways with great spirit.

"What makes you say that?" he asked.

"Because it's *the* thing to say on these occasions," she replied. "Go on—' in thus setting at defiance all rules of etiquette and propriety; but as you *have* done it, it's no use making a fuss about it, and I forgive you. You'd better go and be married at the Embassy Chapel as soon as possible. I will arrange about the licence in London, and will telegraph to Lord Mountchessington at Paris.

'Your affectionate uncle,
'MALDON.'"

"I don't know that I mean to do all this," said the Duke. "Your mother will be furious at my connivance at it. She swears she'll clap her in a penitentiary the minute she comes into England!"

"But you *will* write it," said Lady George. "I know you will. It really isn't respectable for the family—your niece gadding about the Continent in this sort of way, like a—a——Polish Countess!"

"No more it is. I'll write the letter, and another one to Parchment to tell him to get the licence; and one to Mountchessington. That'll set the whole thing straight. I shan't tell your mother what I have done; there'll be no peace if I do!"

"Where's Dagenham? In the garden still?"

"Yes; he's standing out there by the fountain: he's got a rose in his hand, which he's pulling to pieces."

"He's making the offer," said the Duke, going to the window.

"And she'll refuse him."

"What makes you think that?"

"Because I know she's head-over-ears in love with her cousin!"

"I never could see the fun of cousins marrying. It's the next mild thing to marrying your grandmother, which the Prayer-book sternly forbids the rising genetion to *think* of ever. Who the devil would want to?—it's quite an unnecessary precaution, in my opinion. I never, even in my young days, felt the slightest inclination to do it."

"Or anybody else, I should think!" replied Lady George. "I never felt any *penchant* for my grandfather—then, to be sure, he was a crusty old chap! so perhaps that accounts for it."

"Perhaps it does," said his Grace, who could hardly speak for laughing; "perhaps it does!"

Over the breakfast-room at Maldon Lodge is the Duchess's boudoir: it is rather limited in space, but it is beautifully furnished, and the mirrors on the walls multiply everything till the idea almost of "vastness" is conveyed. The Duchess and Sir John Fenacre were standing at the window, watching Lord Dagenham and Madeleine.

Both were agitated to the utmost degree. The Duchess wanted the match on account of the money, and the Baronet for the position it would give his daughter, and through him the glory it would shed over him individually, as the father of a Duchess. It was an anxious time for both of them. They both knew by *instinct* that Dagenham was making an offer, and they were both equally anxious for different reasons that his suit should be successful.

Sir John fidgeted first on one leg and then on another; he did not know what to do or say. It crossed his mind that there was a bare possibility of her saying "No," and he turned pale with terror at the thought.

The Duchess was not very sanguine as to the success of her son's love-making: she knew that there was an "affair" in the way. "Really," she had said to her husband, "girls who have got money and are not in the market should have a board round their necks with 'ENGAGED' on it: it's such a disappointment to a young man, when he's had all the bother of making love, to find that there is a previous attachment!"

They both stood by the window, and both knew what was uppermost in each other's thoughts, but they discussed on different subjects, such as the weather, or the papers, all the while keeping their eyes fixed on the pair by the fountain.

"That niece of mine is a sad ungrateful girl," said the Duchess, "after all the kindness I have shown her. It's a deplorable example of the lamentable depravity of the human race."

"The old Adam," murmured Sir John. "The old Adam!"

"True," said her Grace, with a sigh. "On such natures as hers, all love and tenderness is thrown away. I have been like a mother to her, and this is the reward I get; this is her gratitude!"

"Ah, indeed," said Sir John, who was getting so nervous and fidgety he could hardly stand still.

"I am determined that her folly and ingratitude shall meet with the punishment it deserves. I'm her legal guardian, and I wont give my consent to a marriage. When people begin to point at her, and shrug their shoulders, on her return to London, she will feel bitterly the madness of the step she has taken, and may perhaps by that time have sufficiently repented to go and be a "sister," or something of that sort. I don't mind paying the entrance-fee to the Lady Superior, if she is a strict disciplinarian."

The Duchess of Maldon felt very virtuous when she said all this. It is the very quintessence of delight to some people when they can make the consequence of indiscretion *felt.* She quite gloated over the idea of the retribution with which Minnie would be visited on her return to London, and the poignant shame she would feel when people " cut" her in the " Row." The world is so very virtuous, it *never* does anything wrong—the fact is, that it sins with such cunning that it is not found out.

When a " worldling" less skilled in the art of dissimulation than his fellows, has his life laid bare, all the others come and peck at him like crows round carrion. " It's *so* shocking!" say the Messrs. and Mesdames

Whited-Sepulchre. "Such *fearful* disclosures! so *very* sad!"

Meanwhile, Lord Dagenham and Madeleine were standing by the fountain. She was feeding the gold fish with crumbs, and staring intently into the water.

"How calm and peaceful everything seems this morning!" said Dagenham.

"Yes."

"I sometimes think I should like to pass my life in these solitudes, far away from the busy hum of cities, and glide gently down the stream of time, till the current bore me to the haven of rest."

"It would be an enjoyable, but a useless life," said Madeleine. "And life doesn't seem given to us to dream it away; we ought to *do* something in our generation, and not pass away without leaving some trace of our existence behind us!"

"It's a noble ambition to leave a name,

and yet I do not care to enter into the vortex of public or political life."

" Your position requires you to do it; rank has responsibilities which ought to be acted up to."

" You are like a second Socrates, Miss Fenacre, and I must acknowledge that your way of looking on life is the right one. I don't care for success for myself; if I had some one to take an interest in my schemes, and at whose feet I could lay my laurels, it would be different, but as it is I don't care for it."

'· You have your family ?"

" They don't take any interest in me or my doings. I was born into the world, in their estimation, for the simple purpose of becoming Duke of Maldon, and what I may do individually as a man, or achieve by my own exertions, is looked upon as a secondary consideration."

"You should break through that idea, and carve out a way for yourself."

"I would if I had some one who'd rejoice at my success, or mourn my failure with me."

"Your friends would do that."

"I don't mean with the cold sympathy of friendship. I mean something nearer and dearer—the sympathy of love. Madeleine, I love you with all my heart, with all my soul, with all my strength. Can you love me?"

"No, I cannot."

"Oh, Madeleine! You will kill me if you say that again."

"I cannot."

"You love another?"

"Yes."

"Then there is no hope for me! My life will henceforth be miserable and wasted! All the bright dreams of future happiness are dashed for ever to the ground!"

"Don't speak of your life in that way. It's only a feeling of despair that will soon pass away. You will find some one more worthy of your love than I."

[This is a modest speech not often made on such occasions.]

"Impossible! My existence will henceforth be a pathless ocean, without the compass of hope. Madeleine, good-bye. I cannot stay here any longer. Good-bye."

"We part friends? You are not angry with me?"

"Angry with you! No; how could I be?"

"Then we will be henceforth as brother and sister to each other—nothing more. Good-bye."

Lord Dagenham walked slowly to the house, every now and then repeating to himself, "Brother and sister—nothing more."

Madeleine went on throwing crumbs to the gold fish.

"I'd bet a 'pony,'" said Lady George, "that Dagenham's got his *congé*."

"Impossible!" said the Duke. "The girl would never be such a fool."

"Yes she would. Didn't I tell you that she was in love with her cousin?"

"Yes. But if she was, she'd throw him over for Dagenham. Your mother threw over Mr. Beaufoy for me."

"But then she's what Whitey Brown calls a 'worldling,' and Madeleine isn't."

"True," said the Duke. "If any one *is*, she is a 'thoroughbred,' and nothing else."

The Duke was fond of the "turf," and used nothing but Newmarket phraseology in the affairs of every-day life.

The Duchess of Maldon and Sir John, in the boudoir, both knew, by intuitive feelings, that Madeleine had been proposed to and had said "No;" but they did not give utterance to the thought.

"The sun's very hot for Madeleine to stand out of the shade so long," said the Duchess.

"I'll go and tell her to come in," said Sir John. Then he went and took his hat, and strolled out on to the lawn.

"What have you and Dagenham been talking about?"

"Nothing," said Madeleine.

"Then you had a good deal to say about it, that's all. Answer me this one question. Has he made you an offer or not?"

"He has."

"And you said yes, of course?"

"I said *No*."

Sir John was petrified—breathless. He was some few minutes before he could speak. In his emotion and agitation he nearly fell into the basin of the fountain.

"Can I believe my ears? Say it again. *What* did you answer my Lord Viscount Dagenham?"

"I said *No.*"

Sir John stared, and was speechless.

"Are you mad? Do you know *what* you are refusing?—the oldest ducal coronet in England; a splendid position; a magnificent jointure; a nearly regal establishment. You must be mad!" Then Sir John said, very slowly and deliberately, "Do you mean to say you will not marry the heir-apparent to all this? Answer me!"

"No," said Madeleine, looking him full in the face; "no."

Sir John Fenacre fainted dead away.

CHAPTER VIII.

SIR JOHN IN PARIS.

"Ambition was my idol, which was broken
Before the shrines of sorrow and of pleasure;
And the two last have left me many a token,
O'er which reflection may be made at leisure."
BYRON.

THE Englishman in Paris is not what he was in the days of the First Empire. In those benighted times, he was a "milord" to the Parisians, and a mine of wealth on account of his conceit and gullibility. He knew little or nothing of the language, manners, or customs of the country he was visiting; but, for all that, like a true Briton, he pretended he did, and was fleeced and shorn to an amazing extent by the sharpwitted Gauls. An hotelkeeper in those days put up in his window, "English spoken here." And if he could repeat the national "damn" with tolerable fluency, he was pretty sure of securing a tolerable amount of English custom. But "*Nous avons changé tout cela,*" and most travelling Britons have a knowledge of the French tongue, or, at all events, a slight smattering of their "cursed lingo," as old comedy heroes express it. And it is as unromantic a feat to run over to Paris by the "tidal express," as to go to South Kensington in a hansom.

After Madeleine had refused Lord Dagenham, Sir John Fenacre thought it best to put his long deferred project of going abroad into execution. So accordingly, after spending a week in London over the necessary preparations for a somewhat lengthy sojourn on the Continent, he had left Charing Cross one evening by the tidal train, and next morning found himself in the French capital

"Bless me!" he had exclaimed, on driving through the streets to his hotel, "how the place has altered!"

Sir John had not been in Paris for thirty years, and consequently found it *had* altered. The French are not a nation to stand still, or remain stationary either in science, art, manufactures, or architecture; on the contrary, they are what the Americans call "go-a-head"—that is to say, they do not hold the "what-was-good-enough-for-my-grandmother-is-good-enough-for-me" theory, which I hold to be a most pernicious and preposterous one.

The day after his arrival in Paris, Sir John had left cards at the English Embassy. He knew Lord Mountchessington in former days, and felt no scruple in claiming his acquaintance.

His maxim was, never to suffer an acquaintance who might be useful to relapse into a stranger, or a friend to fall into the position of an acquaintance. "You never know when you may want them," he used to say; "and some people are so confoundedly high and mighty, that they pretend they don't recognise you just at the moment you do want them." Before he succeeded to the baronetcy he had plenty of experience of this sort; men who had made their way did not see any particular use in knowing John Fenacre; so, accordingly, they *did not* know him. But he, nothing daunted, would walk up to them in high places, and shake them cordially by the hand, all the while hating them in his heart. He was totally impervious to the most *prononcé* " cut ;" he would smile affably

and benignly on the "cutter," and would
retaliate by calling men familiarly by their
surnames, without the awful prefix of Mr. or
"My Lord!" He knew the private history of
most of the Peerage and half the Commons;
and woe betide those exalted personages if
they "cut" John Fenacre. He would immediately call on his whole acquaintance, and
retail, with sundry additions of his own,
some of the most "startling disclosures in
high life" that ever followed the heading
of that sensational paragraph in the papers.
People knew that he *knew*, or said he did,
more than they liked to have published;
therefore, as a rule, they had been civil to
him, even before he was "Sir" John, or
there was the remotest reason for taking
any notice of him whatever.

This was all changed now, and as the
owner of the Grange, and a Baronet, he
received the consideration for which he had

been thirsting all his life. His one idea now was "place," and he was prepared to go any length to obtain it. There was to be a general election the following spring, and he would *sit* for Fenacre.

When Sir John said he would *sit* for Fenacre, he *did* mean he would *stand* for that borough. The bare possibility of any one daring to contest it never crossed his mind. For centuries the "free and independent burgesses" had returned a Fenacre or a nominee of that family, and Sir John firmly believed that they would continue to do so for all time. Whether he was justified in the supposition we shall see at a future period of this history; for the present we will follow his movements in Paris.

I have said that he left cards at the Embassy, and an answer had been vouchsafed in the shape of an intimation that Lady

Mountchessington was "At home" on certain specified occasions.

The Baronet was sitting over the breakfast-table in his apartments in the Rue St. Honoré, and his daughter was sitting opposite to him.

"Here are cards for the Embassy 'At home,'" said Sir John.

"I suppose they are very like the same things in London," replied Madeleine, "and I am sure I got heartily sick of them this season."

"There you are!" said Sir John, testily; "you never like anything—you women are all alike. You bother, bother to get a thing, and when you *have* got it, why, you say you don't care about it! You said you wanted to come abroad, and the first thing that turns up to be done you wont do it!"

Then he rustled the pages of *Galignani*, and began to read steadily.

"I didn't say I wouldn't go," said Madeleine; "I merely said I didn't care about it."

"It's all the same thing—you never like anything I do!"

"Indeed, papa, you are quite wrong. I'll go to the Embassy with you with the greatest pleasure. It's not fair of you to say that!"

Sir John had not recovered his daughter's "confounded folly and nonsense" in refusing a Duke's *eldest* son. "By Jove, the best match in England!" Lady George, by way of comforting him, had spoken of Lord Dagenham being subject to fits. "Hang his fits!" he had replied; "I don't care *that* about them!"

Then he snapped his fingers, which is an embodiment of the sentiment "that."

Just then one of the waiters came up to the table and began, in broken English, to ask whether "Milord" would have "encore another cup of corfay?"

"Parlays-fransay?" said Sir John, looking at him sternly. " Confound the fellow! does he think I am an ignorant snob who doesn't understand the French language!" Then he continued, with dignity, " Parlay-fransay, Mossoo!"

"Ah! oui, monsieur. Parle Français?" said the waiter.

" Parlay-fransay!" exclaimed Sir John. " Of course I do."

" Voulez-vous encore une tasse de café, une omelette, ou des œufs, monsieur?"

"Oui; je no comprendy," replied Sir John.

The waiter repeated his sentence.

" Oui; portez-moi—encore—une—œuf?"

"Que-voulez-vous, monsieur?"

"Confound the fellow! he can't speak his own language: he *positively* can't speak his own language. Never met with anything like it in my life—never!"

Then he leant back in his chair, and laughed heartily.

Madeleine seeing the evident confusion of the poor waiter, charitably told him what her father *did* want, in very fair French.

"What did you say to that grinning jackanapes of a Frenchman?" asked the Baronet.

"I told him what you wanted."

"Told him what I wanted! Told him what I wanted! Why, I told him myself, and that's enough, I suppose."

"But he didn't understand you!"

"That was his confounded stupidity— nothing else but his confounded stupidity. I suppose you will say it was *mine* next?"

He was fast working himself into a rage.

"You mean to say I didn't speak his cursed lingo correctly?" he continued.

"Well, it was rather unintelligible."

"Rather unintelligible! Rather unintelligible, was it?" Then he sneered, and repeated, "*Rather* unintelligible! A pretty thing for a daughter to tell her father that what he says is 'rather unintelligible.' I suppose you'll say I am a fool next? Upon my word, I shouldn't be in the *least* surprised if you *were* to call me a fool! Bless my soul! what is the world coming to? I should have liked to have seen *my* father's face if I'd called *him* a fool. I *may* say, I should like to have seen it!" This last he said very slowly, with great deliberation, and with a peculiar emphasis on the words "may say."

"I didn't say so," said Madeleine.

"But you think it, and it's all the same. You really are the most undutiful girl that a father was ever plagued with."

Then he nearly cried over his paper, and felt a kind of choking in his throat. He was thinking of that little affair by the fountain, in the grounds of Maldon Lodge, N.B.

Madeleine got up and put her arms round his neck and kissed him: she actually felt for the poor man's disappointment in not seeing her affianced to a Duke's *eldest* son.

Her feeling was what may be termed, according to papistical phraseology, a work of supererogation."

"Go away!" said Sir John. "Go away!"

"Don't be so cross with me," said Madeleine.

"Go away!" repeated the Baronet. "You always manage to get round me. I am a foolish, soft-hearted old fool!—that's what I am, and give you a dev'lish sight too much your own way. There now—go along with you!"

Then he returned her embrace. His wrath did not last long: it was merely transitory and passing, like an April shower; and then he had been stirred to the very depths by

Madeleine's preposterous conduct at Maldon Lodge, N.B.

"We'll go and see some of the 'sights,'" said Sir John. "Garçong. Allez—cherches un voiter!"

"Oui, monsieur," said the waiter; then left the room to execute the order.

Sir John was delighted at being understood at once. "You wont say I can't parlay-fransay with the best of them now!" he exclaimed. "By Jove, I know their lingo better than they do themselves!"

"La voiture vous attende au portecochère!"

"Bong," said Sir John; "let it attend jusqua mamselle—hab—habil. Confound it! Get her, what-do-you-call-it, chapeau, et her, her, her——"

"Parapluie, monsieur?"

"Ah! oui — yes. I wonder what the devil a 'perpleu' is? I'll ask Madeleine when

I get in the carriage. ' Perpleu—perpleu!'" he kept repeating to himself. "I suppose it's a shawl or jacket, or something of that sort. Oui, mossoo!" he said to the waiter. "Jusqua mamselle supporte son perpleu! By Jove! I wish Madeleine was here to hear me parlaying-fransay like this, absolutely with as good an accent as a native!"

I am afraid Sir John was rather over-rating his powers when he gave utterance to this latter panegyric on his conversational abilities. Much to his relief, Madeleine made her appearance, as he was rapidly losing himself amidst the meshes and quicksands of the French language.

"Where shall we go first?" he asked, as they got into the carriage.

"Oh, the Tuileries!" replied his daughter.

"Toolereys," said the Baronet, majestically, to the porter, as he shut the door. "Dites au choshay allez au Toolereys."

"Bien, monsieur!" replied the porter, without betraying the least semblance of merriment. If it had been a Frenchman in England murdering our language, a man of that class would burst out laughing in his face. But the French are more polite.

It is not a very long drive from the Rue St. Honoré to the Tuileries, and Sir John and Madeleine were soon at the Palace. The chief fault found with the exterior of the building is, that the roof is too heavy and too high for the façade of the building; and the extraordinary crowding of statues and busts in the embellishment gives it altogether an appearance of over-elaboration and ponderousness. But however, it is no part of the present writer to discuss the merits of the architecture of the Tuileries; it is merely his province to record the visit of Sir John and Miss Fenacre.

The associations of the Tuileries are

identical with those of the two great eras in French history, namely, the Louis Quatorze and Napoleonic. Both these great men made the Tuileries their constant residence while in Paris, and the descendant of the latter, well knowing the importance of prestige, especially with an impressionable nation like the French, has likewise adopted it as his town house.

It was about half an hour before noon, and the gardens were rapidly becoming crowded with the good people of Paris, who make it their custom to walk there in the morning, or rather sit on chairs and see other people do it.

Sir John and Madeleine were walking before the row of chairs, and were being freely criticised by the messieurs and mesdames. Madeleine was what is called a "showy" looking girl, and beside, had a *chevelure* of the colour so immensely admired by the French, chiefly on account of its rarity in their country—at least, its rarity as a *natural* beauty; there are plenty of golden tresses produced by art in Paris as well as in other places. In fact, it was in that capital that the idea was first started that we might, on paying a certain fixed sum, be made " Beautiful for ever," and like other things, it was produced in London as a new idea, when it had become quite hackneyed in Paris.

" I wonder who that girl is?" said a young Englishman, as he passed.

" What do you want to know for?" said a lady, whom, by her likeness, must have been his mother.

" Because hers is a face I have seen in my dreams, but never before saw realized," he replied.

" How absurdly sentimental you are! You are always dreaming."

"Perhaps I am," he replied. "I must get back to my books again: they are the best companions after all: they never contradict or worry one; they are always calm, immovable, unchangeable—which is more than can be said for living friends!"

"There is nothing more deceitful than friendship in the world—except it be love!"

"Not love in its true sense," he replied. "There can be no deception if it is real and heartfelt."

The counterfeit is so very like it, that people are sometimes a long while discovering the alloy in the pure metal!

"Let us go back to the hotel; I am weary of this crowd, with its thoughtless merriment."

"As you like," said his mother.

Then they both left the gardens.

Meanwhile Sir John and Madeleine were walking about amongst the groups of vivacious Parisians. She thoroughly enjoyed the novelty of the scene, and the gaiety and brightness of everything about her.

There is something in the clearness of the atmosphere abroad, that has a wonderful effect in producing a feeling of elasticity quite different to that experienced under our leaden skies. The influence of the atmosphere is very great, especially as the air becomes lighter and rarefied—so say those who have been "up in a balloon."

On leaving the Tuileries Gardens, they drove to the Invalides, that magnificent asylum of the heroes of France. It was a sublime idea to make the retreat of these veterans the depository of the choicest spoils of war. As they walk beneath the waving war-stained banners, perhaps the trophies of their own valour, every glorious exploit in which they have borne a share must be recalled warm to their memory. They forget their wounds, their age; again they fight the battles of their country; again exult in the shout of victory!

Old veterans are to be seen sitting under the trees, recounting the glories of their youth to a group of ragged urchins; telling them of the battles they have fought, the marches they have made, and the victories they have won, under " *ce cher petit caporal.*"

The principal attraction at the Invalides is, of course, the tomb of Napoléon le Grand, or " Bonaparty," as old men call him. His ashes repose in the midst of the capital of the French people, whom he loved so well. At least, he loved them so well as to make the whole nation a tool to his ambition. And it was only because the glory of France was identical with his glory, that he devoted his life to raising her to the summit of the scale of nations. There was a dark background to his glory—the crowds of miserable conscripts that he drove remorselessly, year after year, into the jaws of death; the desolated fields and the burning homesteads; the tears and groans of widows, orphans, and mothers bereft of those most dear to them! But of course this is all swallowed up in the halo of his success. No one thinks of the *price* he paid for his ascendancy; they only see the *fact* of his power, and applaud.

"Bonaparty was a great man," said Sir John, "but Wellington beat him all to bits. The mounseer wont forget Waterloo in a hurry."

Madeleine was carefully examining the reliques of Napoleon. She thought he was a very great man—almost a demi-god; but then she took the sentimental view of his life.

"I'd answer for it," said Sir John, "that for every person that visits Wellington's tomb in the crypt of St. Paul's, a dozen go and see Bonaparty in Paris."

It might be added that for every person who visits the scenery of his native country, twenty go abroad to see the sights of foreigners. People think nothing in nature is worth the trouble of a visit at home; but they will stare at a millpond abroad with the greatest possible interest.

Having done the Invalides, the Fenacres returned to their hotel. They were going to drive in the Bois in the afternoon, and going to the "Français" in the evening; the night they meant to get rid of at the Embassy's "At home."

The drive in the Bois was not remarkable for anything in particular; except for a slight alteration in the dresses and equipages, it differs in no respect from Hyde Park at five P.M. in the season.

The play at the "Français" was Molière's

" Médecin malgré lui," at which the Baronet laughed heartily, though he did not understand a word of it. He ejaculated, " That's good!" at regular intervals, with great gusto.

One of the occupants of the stalls kept his *lorgnettes* on the Baronet's box for some time, till at last he remarked it, and took up his, and tried to " look" him down. When he got the right focus, he started. " We wont stay for the afterpiece," he said to Madeleine.

CHAPTER IX.

MADELEINE MAKES A CONQUEST.

" Yet was there light around her brow,
A holiness in those dark eyes,
Which show'd—tho' wandering earthward now—
Her spirit's home was in the skies."

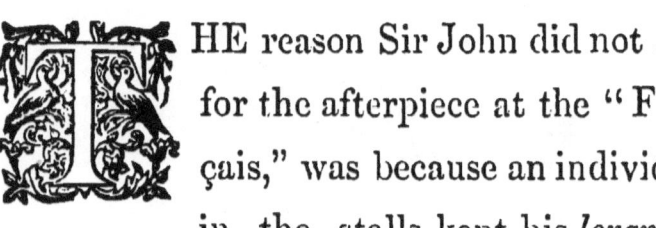HE reason Sir John did not stay for the afterpiece at the "Français," was because an individual in the stalls kept his *lorgnettes* persistently on his box, and the Baronet recognised in him a person whom he particularly wished to avoid. However, in this he was destined to be disappointed; for, directly he got into the vestibule of the Embassy, he recognised him leaning against

one of the pillars. The Baronet made no remark, but hurried on to the reception room. He was well received by Lady Mountchessington; and it was a kind of unction to his soul to bask in the smiles of Madame l'Ambassadrice.

We had the last scene of Lady George's theatricals here," said her ladyship. " Paris and la belle Hélène were married at the Embassy Chapel this morning."

"Bless me!" ejaculated the Baronet. " The Duchess said she would never consented to it!"

" I suppose she has relented, because my husband had a letter from the Duke about it only two days ago."

" Very extraordinary! She declared to me that nothing would induce her to consent to it. Absolutely nothing!"

" I suppose she took a lady's privilege— and altered her mind."

"She must have had some very strong reasons!"

"Perhaps she knows nothing about it. Husbands don't always show their wives every letter they write."

"I don't think the Duke would do it without telling her. She would be perfectly furious when she heard of it."

"He said that he and Lady George both thought it the best thing to be done under the circumstances. He did not mention his wife."

"Then you may depend upon it she knows nothing whatever about it."

"Then she'll know it to-morrow, because it will be in the papers," said her ladyship.

"You made great havoc that night, Miss Fenacre, in your twofold attributes of goddess of beauty and love. In the first case, by bewitching mankind in general; and in the second, by inspiring two young people with the idea that they were in love, and must perpetrate matrimony there and then!"

Madeleine blushed, and denied having the slightest knowledge of the *dénouement* of the theatricals.

Then Lady Mountchessington left them to make a tour of the room, leaning on the arm of that celebrated French diplomatist, M. le Prince de Santerre.

After her ladyship's departure, Lord Mountchessington came up, and shook Sir John cordially by the hand.

"Glad to see you!" he said; "and Miss Fenacre too. By-the-by, there's a young Englishman been asking to be introduced to you—a Mr. Raynor. But here he comes. Mr. Raynor," said the Ambassador, "I shall be most happy to introduce you to Miss Fenacre." Then he went on talking to Sir John.

Mr. Raynor immediately asked Madeleine to dance, and she accepted.

"What do you think of the Tuileries?" said he. "I saw you in the garden this morning."

"Oh! I like it immensely. Such a grand old place, and associated with so much that is great and glorious!"

"Are you going to remain in Paris long?"

"Only a week or ten days longer; then we are going to Heidelberg."

"Heidelberg! I'm going to Heidelberg. I'm going to study at the University there."

"Oh, indeed. Are you going to plunge into the depths of German philosophy and metaphysics, till you become so sceptical that you'll believe in nothing?"

"I hope not the latter part; but I hope to obtain some insight in the former."

"One leads to the other very often. People

get lost in the mazes of speculation and abstruseness till they have not a firm spot left to fix their faith to!"

" Why ! have you dived into those unknown depths yourself, and come out a cynic ?"

" No; but I have read a good deal on the subject of 'speculative theories,' and what I said just now is the conclusion I have come to. Thank you, I'll stop here."

Then she bowed, and took up a position by Sir John's side.

" Who is that you were dancing with?" asked her father.

" A Mr. Raynor."

" Don't dance with him again."

" Why not?"

" Don't ask why. It's enough for you to know I forbid it."

Madeleine stared at him with astonishment. What possible reason could there be against dancing with a young man who had been introduced to her by the Ambassador. She couldn't make it out at all.

"We'll go now," said Sir John; "these 'At homes' are attended by so many questionable characters, that they are not fit places for young ladies of good family."

When he said of "good family," he meant the Fenacres *par excellence*. The Fenacres had been "in" before the Conqueror; they were remotely descended from Adam, and as he was the first man, one cannot well boast a more ancient pedigree, unless we give in to the pre-Adamite theory. If there *were* pre-Adamites, we do not know what their names were, so they cannot figure on our "blazoned scroll of fame."

"We'll go to St. Cloud to-morrow, and perhaps Versailles the next day. Then we might as well get on; I am getting tired of Paris."

"Very well," replied Madeleine. "Good night."

Then she climbed the staircase to her apartment, which was situated on the third floor. When she reached her room, she threw herself on the sofa, and indulged in that delightful feeling the French call *rêverie*, or in more matter-of-fact English parlance, a retrospect.

Of course the first person she thought of was Loftus; she was, or fancied herself to be, very much in love with him. Then she fancied that she liked Lord Dagenham— just a little bit—but not enough to marry him, of course. But all the same, if he was to ask her again, she really did not know what she should say, "Yes" or "No!" Then she thought of Loftus, and decided under any circumstances she would have said the latter. Then Mr. Raynor at the Embassy that night, and her father's unaccountable prohibition of her speaking to him—she could not make it out at all.

That he *had* a reason she did not doubt. Sir John was a man who had a reason for everything he did or said out of the common way; but, like a wise and discreet "worldling," he kept it to himself till the proper moment arrived for divulging it.

That this Mr. Raynor was somehow or other connected with a former phase of the Baronet's life, Madeleine did not doubt. He had formerly been on intimate terms with people whom he would now cut dead in the street if he met them. Prosperity is a wonderful obliterator of past friendships with people who are going down in the world, instead of climbing upwards. When a man has made " Excelsior" his motto, he forgets those who are left behind—as long as he comes in *first*, he does not care whether his friends are a bad third, or *nowhere.* He becomes straightway an egotist, and wraps himself in a proof mail of *self.*

We will change the scene to the dormitory of the worthy Baronet. He was sitting in his dressing-gown and slippers before a small fire; the autumn evenings were getting cold. "That young cub," he said to himself, " didn't recognise me—doesn't know me by sight even, though I do him. The old woman is not far off, I warrant. He's just like poor Richard was at his age, as like as two peas! I suppose he *did* marry that woman; only they all tell such lies that you never know when to believe them! Parchment advises me to keep quiet about it, and he knows what he's about; that forty thousand *was* a sum to stump-up!" Then he sighed, and continued, "But it is better than losing the whole concern though—by Jove, it is!"

And with this sentiment he retired to bed, and was soon in the land of Nod, wherever that may be.

Sir John Fenacre's position was a peculiar one, and before we judge him too harshly, we ought to look at what are called, whether rightly or not is another question, " extenuating circumstances."

He comes into the estate, and finds that the late proprietor had made a will assigning all the available personalty to his housekeeper. He strongly suspects that a marriage has taken place between the two parties, the testator and the legatee, but he has no *proof* of it! If it is true, why does not the heir claim the baronetcy? Would any man in his senses neglect to prefer his claim to an estate of seven thousand a year, unless he knew that his claim would not not bear investigation and proof? Up to the day of the funeral, Sir John had never had a suspicion that his brother had ever been married previously to his union with Eleanor Forrester, and therefore why was *he* to institute an inquiry; his part was surely the *defence*, not the attack! People surely cannot expect a man to calmly and deliberately commence the operation known in vulgar parlance as "cutting his own throat." It was not the first time that claims have been made to an estate which had no more stable foundation than the fertile imagination of the claimant, and therefore why should not this be a similar case? We know that in the heat of the moment Sir John had exclaimed, "It's just like the abominable race of women to have a son, and say it was poor Richard's." And in his calmer moments he comforted himself with the same theory.

The Psalmist said in his haste, " All men are liars." Sir John at his leisure said the same of all women. It was a consolation to him to think it, and hope devoutly that *one* in particular would keep up the sweeping anathema he had passed on the whole sex, and not attempt to shame her sisters by setting up for an exception to the general rule.

Having seen Sir John and Madeleine both "tucked-up" in their respective apartments for the night, we will leave the Rue St. Honoré for the Boulevards of the metropolis of gaiety, as Paris has been termed.

Though it is far advanced in the small hours of the night, the Parisians are by no means under the influence of Morpheus. On the contrary, the gaslights stream from the windows of the brilliantly-illuminated cafés, and a subdued hum of voices is heard through the glass doors. There are not many people walking about, bar the inevitable *gendarmes* who form a feature in every scene of French town life.

The licensed orgies of the Palais Royal are no more, but in their place has cropped up a growth of abominations which minister to the vicious tastes of the inhabitants of one of the most dissolute capitals in Europe.

Alured Raynor was lounging on the Boulevards; he ought to have been in bed, of course, but he was not. He was smoking a cigar, and, as it was cold, had wrapped himself in a long black Spanish cloak. If he had been in love with Madeleine before he was introduced to her, he was now in that desperate state termed " over head and ears." He felt he could neither rest nor remain quiet for a moment till he had seen her again.

There is something very curious in the mysterious effects extreme agitation of the mind has on the body. It may be termed the triumph of the spiritual over matter.

Under the influence of some great mental excitement, the body is fused into unison with the purpose of the soul. It becomes capable of sustaining an extraordinary amount of fatigue without any of the symptoms of exhaustion or paralysation which it would experience on ordinary occasions.

It was so with Alured Raynor; he felt too agitated to remain quiet or stationary. The only way of securing anything like mental calmness was to keep up a kind of "perpetual motion." He was madly—devotedly—in love; in love as one is only *once* in a lifetime; with an ardour that cannot be experienced *twice*. Who would eat hashed venison who could get the haunch? or who would care to drink champagne that was opened yesterday? Bah! the only thing that makes it worth having is the freshness and sparkle; and that is all gone on the second day! The only charm of love is *novelty*, and when that is gone, away flies romance and sentiment, and leaves in its place income-tax and perambulators, butchers' bills and water-rates!

This was Alured Raynor's *first* love, and consequently he was utterly and hopelessly dazzled and infatuated. Besides, till he was introduced to Madeleine he didn't know her *name*, and when he heard it the recoil of his feelings had been most poignant. That he should love the daughter of a house he hated, and whose head he was! Oh, the foul stain of that one dark night! Rivers of tears and repentance could never wash away that black damning blot! There it was, and there it ever would be, indelibly marked with a red-hot brand. The iron had entered into his soul. He was seared with a sense of guiltiness! He had never felt it till now, and when he contrasted himself stained with sin, to Madeleine in her spotless purity, he felt it would be the very acme of selfishness to dare to hope that she would link her lot with such as he, so utterly unworthy of her as he was.

Alured Raynor had the rare grace of humility. At least, *my* experience of the world tells me it *is* rare; I do not know what may be the general opinion on the subject. He was also unselfish enough to have scruples about attempting to drag Madeleine down to his level; there would be fewer of the marriages which serve to propagate a breed of paupers if all men were as unselfish in their love!

If a man really loves a woman he shows it, of course, by persuading her to quit the substantial comforts of her father's house, with a sufficiency of food and raiment, and opportunities of enjoying the pleasures of social intercourse, diversified by the delights of the opera and concert-room, for a "three-pair back," with a minimum of loaves and fishes, and a scanty dole of pleasure, the compensation being his delightful society. Oh, noble and unselfish man! To tell the truth, this is not the stupendous sacrifice that it appears at first sight. " Lor bless you!" as the angler said when he was baiting his hooks with worms in spite of their wriggling, " they like it!"

We do *not* know whether the angler is right about the worms; we think he is not; but we *know* that his remark applies to the daughters of Eve, who, to give them their due, are *perfectly* unselfish when they love! —not so the lords of the creation. For every henpecked husband, there are twenty wives who suffer in a life-long bondage to that tyrant called man!—they suffer in silence, and weep in solitude, but they will go on trusting their happiness to him as long as the world lasts. Was not Eve made for Adam's gratification, and did not she immediately lead him astray?

The hubbub and din of Paris is at length subsided, but only for an hour or two: the brisk sound of *réveille* will soon be screaming from a hundred bugles, for Paris is a military city, and the French a military people. They have their beloved troops in the midst of them; they are proud of them, and like to see the gallant sons of Mars in all the glory of gold lace and red breeches, in their streets and gardens, flirting with the *bonnes*.

We English, on the contrary, like our "gallant defenders" better at a distance. Dire are the wails if some devoted place is fixed upon by the War Office for a garrison town! No one is pleased but the beershop proprietor, who sees a golden harvest in view. English people like military glory, but have no idea of fêteing or petting *les militaires.* Every one hates garrison towns but young ladies whose charms are on the wane, and who, in despair, spread nets for unwary subs. Poor things! they are not often successful, for the British soldier "loves and he rides away." Like King Solomon, he divides his attentions amongst a vast number of ladies.

This is a long digression from the *dramatis personæ* of my story, but my readers must pardon me, as they have the benefit of my opinion on things in general thereby.

The morning's sun had gilded the roofs of Paris some hours when Sir John and his daughter met at breakfast. After interchanging the usual salutations, the Baronet informed her that he meant to visit St. Cloud, and have a kind of picnic in the park there.

Madeleine expressed her acquiescence, and began to pour out the tea.

"Ha!" said Sir John, who was reading the paper; "bless me! what a rage the Duchess will be in to be sure." Then he read out loud, "On — inst., at the Chapel of the British Embassy, Paris, Charles Fitzcharles, of the 4th Regiment Life Guards Green, to the Honourable Marian Snowdrop, only daughter of the late Lord Aldborough, and niece of the Duke of Maldon. No cards."

"No cards, indeed!" said Sir John. "It would have been a confounded piece of impudence if they had *had* them. Bless me!"

Sir John chanted a perpetual Benedicite on himself on all occasions.

"I think the Duchess being so unkind to her made her run away," remarked Madeleine.

"It's no excuse whatever," said Sir John; "none whatever. If she had stuck pins into her, it would be no justification for her atrocious conduct!"

"I believe Lady George knew all about it the night of the theatricals," said Madeleine.

"I have no doubt she did," replied the Baronet. "We'll spend a long day at St. Cloud," he continued. "I remember a verse Walter Scott wrote about it in '15, after the Peace. Here it is:

> 'Few happy hours poor mortals pass,
> Then give those hours their due;
> And rank amongst the foremost class
> Our evenings at St. Cloud.'

I used to know yards of verses once. I was in full chase of a widow, a regular bluestocking! George!" she expected me to know Homer, Virgil, Racine, Tasso, Dante, Rochefoucauld, and the whole of them. So I used to coach up the well known bits one sees quoted in the papers every day—it was all she knew herself—and she thought I was a regular Plato, or some old buffer of that sort!"

Then Sir John leant back in his chair and laughed heartily at the reminiscences of his "widow hunt." "I am glad she stole away, now," said the Baronet; "but it was different then." The Baronet referred to the days of his pecuniary embarrassment. There were lots of things he did then that he would not dream of doing now.

Becky Sharp said a long course of Three per Cents. made her feel virtuous, and I think there is great truth in her remarks. Did not she end her days between Bath and Cheltenham in an halo of pew cushions and hassocks? Did not she go to church on Saints' days, and *never* without a footman? All this was the effect of Three per Cents; if she had not had them she would most likely have gone on at Pumpernickel, leading a life that would not bear a very close inspection, but as it was, she lived in great repute at the city of Bladud! *Moral.*—We should *all* be virtuous if we *could*, and Three per Cents. are highly conducive to that end. Carried *nem. con.*

CHAPTER X.

SISTER MONICA.

"Who can endure the livery of a nun,
For aye to be in shady cloister mew'd?"
SHAKSPEARE.

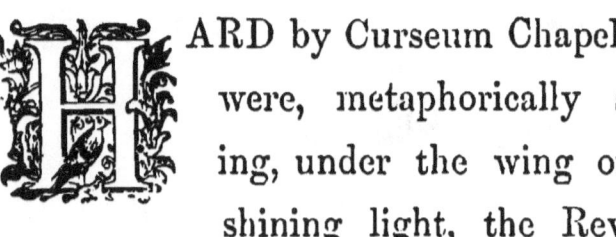ARD by Curseum Chapel, as it were, metaphorically speaking, under the wing of that shining light, the Reverend White Brown, is the Convent of our Lady of Sighs. It is peopled by a reverend mother and twelve sisters, all living under the strictest vows of mortification and abstinence, of perpetual seclusion and abstraction from the world, and one and all having a holy horror of "externs."

In these latter times, it is the fashion to imitate the benighted followers of the beast as closely as possible, and to keep up a close flirtation with the scarlet lady. " Going over to Rome" does not make such a stir now as it used to; the ritualists approach so near to the city on seven hills, that the change is scarcely perceptible by the uninitiated.

If each sister were to tell the truth to her father confessor, when he questioned her *why* she had renounced the world, she would reply, "Because I was not fair enough for man. So I was given to God." Only they do not scruple to make a blasphemous use of the *One* name given under heaven, when speaking of the close relationship that exists between them and the church glorified.

The feeling that prompts this self-immurement is akin to that which made the prophets of Baal cut themselves with knives and lancets, in hopes that their bleeding bodies and torn flesh would soften the obdurateness of their God, or that of the Indian fakirs in the present day, who crawl about like reptiles on the parched earth, and degrade the image and likeness in which they were made by their semblance to the beasts which perish.

Mr. Small had communicated to Lady Fenacre the fact that Charles Forrester was singing in the chorus at " Her Highness's." Of this, as we know, she was cognizant, as she had recognised him herself; but Small had been quite unsuccessful in discovering his address.

The truth was, he heard from some of the singers that inquiries were being made about him, so he resolved to throw up his engagement. All he wanted now was to hide himself from every one whom he had

formerly known, and above all from Lady
Fenacre. "I wont let her know I am
living," he said to himself; "it is better
she should think me dead! Dead! of
course, I'm dead. I was drowned in the
Thames!"

Then he laughed a dismal mocking laugh
—one of those laughs which it is not good
to hear: they have the gall of bitterness in
them.

He did not know what to do: he was too
proud to beg. "I know she would give me
money, but I'd rather die than touch it."
In this frame of mind he was wandering
about the streets, aimlessly and purposeless:
he had a kind of hope that he should kill
himself with fatigue and exposure. If an
omnibus had run over him, he would have
liked it rather than otherwise—at least, he
thought he should. At length he reached
Charles Street, Westminster; it was just the

time of the starting of the Abyssinian expedition, and the recruiting sergeants were unusually busy.

There is always a knot of idlers listening to the persuasive eloquence of the recruiting sergeants in Charles Street, Westminster. Their speeches are the most felicitous specimens of word-painting out. Life in the British army, according to these gallant warriors, is one unceasing round of beer and skittles; prize-money is as plentiful as blackberries in June; the change of scene constant and delightful; and after a short period of service, a grateful country pensions off her soldiers for life.

They say nothing of the poisonous West Indian swamps, the arid sandbanks of Africa, and crowded fœtid holds of the transports! It is all gilding and tinsel: there is no sawdust and chalk.

You see one grinning clown hesitating and looking a great stupid mass of indecision. The sergeant sees him too, and directs his harangue especially to him.

After five minutes' eloquence, with a vivid description of the dash Hodge will cut in a red coat, and how all the girls will be mad after him, he slips the Queen's shilling into his hand, and gives him a bunch of ribbons for his cap, and bears him off in triumph to the Fortune of War, where with other raw materials he boozes till he is drafted off to Chatham or Shorncliffe, to be licked into shape.

It was just such a group as I have described that Charles Forrester joined; in spite of his shabby clothes he looked like a gentleman. The sergeant saw this, and commenced at once.

"We want a few fine young men for the Royal Engineers. The work's very easy and genteel, and it's a moral certainty that an intelligent fellow will rise from the ranks."

There was no need for this eloquence in this case, as Charles Forrester was desperate, and willing to do anything.

"I'll enlist and volunteer for Abyssinia," he said to himself. "Perhaps a bullet or a sunstroke will provide for me; as well that way as any other." Then he took her Majesty's shilling, and became a Royal Engineer.

Then he went into the Fortune of War, and was treated by the sergeant.

"You've seen better times, I warrant?" said that worthy. He was a keen observer of human nature was Sergeant Martinet.

"Perhaps I have," replied Forrester.

This was how all trace of him was lost, even to the astute Mr. Small.

Lady Fenacre was crushed with grief he was the only being she really loved.

Her sister, Lady George, felt towards her

"as a sister," of course, but there was no sympathy between them. Lady Fenacre was all heart and feeling, whilst her sister had such an outer crust of worldliness, that it was difficult for those who did not understand her to know that there was a kernel of love and good feeling under that husk of seeming heartlessness. We have seen her conduct to her friend Mrs. Ewart, and know that half the prudes of Vanity Fair would not have held out a little finger in a similar case. Therefore we should not judge her as a heartless woman, though perhaps she takes too little heed of the conventionalities of life and the rules of etiquette, as laid down by society.

"I think I shall leave the world," said Lady Fenacre to her sister.

"Good gracious!" she replied. "Are you going to cut your throat?"

"No; I mean that I shall devote myself

to a life of contemplation; become a sister in the Convent of our Lady of Sighs."

"Oh! one of Whitey Brown's harem? I hope you'll like it," sneered Lady George. "Pray what name will you be known by in 'religion'—as Katinka?"

Then Lady George burst out laughing at her own wit.

"No; Monica. But I wish you wouldn't talk about it in this light way, Lily."

"Most reverend Sister Monica, I humbly beg your pardon. I suppose I may consider myself shrived?" she continued.

"Oh, Lily!" said Lady Fenacre, "please don't."

"Is Whitey the only man allowed on the premises?" asked Lady George; "because if so, the establishment wouldn't suit me."

"The reverend father visits the convent weekly," said Lady Fenacre, "to hear confession."

"What is one young man among so many?" said Lady George, quoting from the pantomime of " Queen Ladybird." " Do you mean to go in for the place of favourite squaw!"

Lady Fenacre began to cry. Lady George, seeing she was really hurt, left off her bantering tone: she was a good-natured woman.

"Seriously speaking," she continued, "how can you possibly imagine that a life of contemplation can be pleasing to God? What merit can there possibly be in keeping within four walls? If you are tired of the round of society—I am myself, sometimes— well and good. Devote your time to something useful; go and visit the poor; make flannel petticoats; cut up greasy mutton at the soup-kitchen; cover the filthy books of the parochial lending library with clean brown holland; take pieces of jelly to old women,—anything; but, for heaven's sake, do not go into Whitey Brown's harem!"

"I have sworn to do it," said Lady Fenacre. "And unless he gives me absolution, I daren't break my vow."

"I wouldn't give a fig for his absolution!"

"I have sworn, and must keep it."

About a fortnight after this conversation Lady Fenacre took the vows of a novice, and became known in "religion" as Sister Monica.

The Convent of our Lady of Sighs is close to Curscum Chapel—in fact, the "sisters" have a private entrance to the chapel where they sit behind a grating in a darkened sepulchral chamber. Irreverent males have likened it to the monkey cage in the "Zoo." Others have said, on coming out, "There's one girl less to-day. I suppose Whitey Brown had her sewn up in a sack, and thrown in the dead of the night into the Serpentine!"

They alluded to Easter practices prevalent amongt the followers of the Prophet, who throws dark-eyed houris into the foaming Bosphorus, if they at all misbehave themselves or become obnoxious in any way to their lords and masters.

At first Monica found a kind of balm to her wounded spirit in the forms of the convent, but they soon became unutterably dreary. In a word, they were *unsatisfying*, the same dismal round of penances and formulæ, never varying by a hair's breadth. The one *excitement* of these immured women was *confession*.

They invented sins for themselves which they had never committed, in order to spin out the time in the confessional. The penitents knelt at the holy father's knees, and poured out the catalogue of their sins. Then he would raise them from their knees and give them the kiss of peace.

Of course it was a *spiritual* kiss, and had nothing earthly about it!

Then he, White Brown, forgave them their sins. And yet he professed to believe in a Bible which says, " Who can forgive sins but God?" It is a strange mystery. Where does the true function of an ambassador for Christ end, and *priestcraft* set in? Who can tell?

As Lady Fenacre was not a *professed* nun, the rules of the Convent were not so stringent in her case. She was allowed occasional interviews with externs; and her letters escaped—or were supposed to escape—the espionage to which those of the other side were subjected. Convent life appears very delightful to sentimental young ladies, whose vivid imagination conjures up pictures of shaded cloisters, with the great swelling notes of the organ pealing through the fretted roof trees; a picturesque costume of serge and white linen, and a rosary dangling from the waist ; and last, but not *least, a love* of a confessor! This is only the popular delusion of these benighted young persons. Frequent *exposés* have proved that a life of petty annoyances, petty jealousies and bickerings, coupled with the most odious system of suspicious talebearing, malice, and spite, has its *fullest* development within the walls of a convent; and, forsooth, it is all done in the name of religion!

It is a curious notion men have conceived of religion, that it consists in a direct violation of all the laws that are implanted in us by the very fact of our being inhabitants of a world framed and fashioned as this is! So far from eliminating the ordinary weaknesses of humanity, it may be fairly questioned whether the life led in convents does not rather encourage sins quite as bad, and certainly quite as mean and degrading, as those which they seek to avoid. What is the worth of self-sacrifice if it can only be achieved by self-degradation? To battle with the world; to take their chance with the rest in resisting the temptations of the "world, the flesh, and the devil;" to go out and face sin, instead of skulking behind stone walls and trying to hide from it, is surely the nobler and better part.

It is an insult to the divine intelligence to interpret the "whole duty" of man or woman to consist in wearing dirty clothes and scrubbing dirty floors! It is as blind and foolish as the Fetish worshipper, who sacrifices his flesh to please his gods. As to the virtue which is *supposed* to lie in self-mortification, it is a large and wide text, too full of "matter" to get to the root of it in the second volume of a novel.

There are those who will always seek beatification by this cheap road; and to the rest we quote the eloquent words of Heinrich Heine:—"Some day or other, when humanity shall have got quite well again, when the body and soul shall have made their peace together, the factitious quarrel which a *false* Christianity has cooked up between them will appear something hardly comprehensible. The fairer and happier generations of holier unions, that will rise up and bloom in the atmosphere of a religion of pleasure, will smile sadly when they think of their poor ancestors whose life was passed in melancholy abstinence from the joys of this beautiful earth, and who faded away into spectres from the mortal compression which they put upon the warm and glowing emotions of sense!"

Or to quote the late Charles Dickens, when writing an account of his visit to the Shaker settlements in America. " I do abhor, and from my soul detest, that bad spirit—no matter by what class it may be entertained —which would strip life of its healthful graces; rob youth of its innocent pleasures; pluck from maturity and age their pleasant ornaments, and make existence but a narrow path towards the grave. That odious spirit, which, if it could have had full scope and sway upon the earth, must have blasted and made barren the imagination of the greatest men, and left them, in their power of raising up enduring images before their fellow-creatures still unborn, no better than the beasts! That in these broad-brimmed hats and very sombre coats—in stiff-necked solemn-visaged piety, in short, no matter what its garb, whether it have the cropped hair, as in a Shaker village; or long nails, as in a Hindoo temple—I recognise the worst amongst the enemies of heaven and earth, who turn their water at the marriage feasts of this poor world, not into wine but gall! If there must be people vowed to crush the harmless fancies and love of innocent gaieties and delights which are a part of human nature—as much a part of it as any other love or hope which is our common portion—let them, for me, stand openly revealed among the ribald and licentious. The very idiots know they are not an immortal race, and will despise them and avoid them readily!"

Heinrich Heine and Charles Dickens, to you I say Amen. And to you, oh nameless writer of a certain article in the *Standard*, I return many thanks for the loan of your ideas on convents, which have served me for an infinity of *padding* in the present chapter. Honour to whom honour is due!

I do not esteem the practice of extracting other men's thoughts, and then palming them off on the public as your *own*, to be in strict accordance with the rule of *meum* and *tuum*.

When Lady Fenacre had been about a week with "our Lady of Sighs," her sister came to see her.

"How do you like it, as far as you have got?" asked Lady George.

"It's not so satisfying as I expected," was her reply.

"I suppose you're not first favourite?"

"If by 'first favourite' you mean that I am suffered to break the rules of discipline, and am absolved from penance, I certainly am not."

"Isn't the confessional great fun? I have a good mind to go into the den myself some day. It would scare old Whitey out of his life if I told him all my thoughts, words, and deeds, and invented what I hadn't done as I went along! When I'm tired of the 'Row' and the opera, I may perhaps just take him up as a new excitement; but I'm *not* tired of it at present!"

"I wonder when you *will* find the joys of the world are hollow and a mere empty show?" said Lady Fenacre.

"Bless your life!" exclaimed her sister, "I found *that* out long ago. But they *distrait* one for the time being. There are not two people in the world who *do* believe in them as a *reality*, they merely engage in them *pour passer le temps!* If they could find anything more satisfying and equally amusing, they would go in for it; but they can't."

"There is the life of contemplation."

"Pooh! I like activity. If I am to contemplate, let it be mankind—not *one* of the species!"

Just then the conversation was interrupted by the clang of the chapel-bell.

"What's that for?" asked Lady George—"dinner?"

"No; mid-day exercise."

"On the tightrope, or in the goose-step?"

Lady Fenacre made no reply, but pulled a duster from her pocket and tied it over her head; then she went down on her knees, and began to crawl towards the door.

Lady George followed her as if she had been some curious specimen of animal newly imported to the Zoo.

"Is this penance?" she asked.

Her sister replied by a sign which showed that she must keep silence, and in a few minutes reached the chapel-door, which was opened noiselessly and closed again. In this way she went up to her appointed seat, a low seat near the altar; it was the penitential stool for the sisters of "our Lady of Sighs."

All this time Lady Fenacre firmly believed she was glorifying God by these senseless mummeries; and many good men and women honestly believe the same. But they are hopelessly blinded and mistaken—erroneously led away and misled.

Lady George was not prepossessed by her visit to "our Lady of Sighs." "It's a perfect farce," she exclaimed; "the most ridiculous monstrosity. I believe White Brown was the man spoken of who should come 'leading captive silly women!'" She repeated this idea of hers several times that day for the amusement of her friends. Some of my readers will not care much for her opinion, for she was one of those lost creatures, the horror of Curseum Chapel and all right-minded persons—a *worldling!*

CHAPTER XI.

MAJOR MANDARIN GETS CHECKMATED.

"He who spreads a net for others, digs
At the same time a pitfall for himself."
SAPIENTISSIMA.

ON the 8th inst., suddenly, at Maldon Castle, Essex, his Grace Charles George Henry, tenth Duke of Maldon, Viscount Dagenham, and Baron Fitzreine in the Peerage of the United Kingdom, and Baron Strontian in that of Scotland, &c. &c.

"Hurrah!" said Pluto—not the black potentate, but Major Mandarin, who bore his cognomen in this nether world—as he read it in the *Times*. "Hurrah!"

Now this was not right of Pluto; nay, it was utterly inexcusable. We should not be glad, or rejoice at the death of an enemy even, and his Grace of Maldon had never stood Major Mandarin in that stead; wherefore then did his heart rejoice when he saw his name in the " first" column? Why? oh! dull and unpenetrating readers, have you forgotten the *post obit* which created such a stir in the noble family of Fitzreine? " But Queen did not sign it," you will say. " Very true," I reply to you: " but Major Mandarin did—at least, not *in propria persona*, but by means of one of the inferior spirits in his Hades, who was an expert in the art of imitating signatures.

There were numerous specimens of Lord Henry's signature in the strong box in Jermyn Street, and directly he read the announcement of the Duke's death, he rang the bell for his satellite, and ordered him to sign the *post obit*.

"Sign that *post obit* of Lord Henry Fitzreine," he had said. "My Lord Duke is no more."

"Very well, sir," replied the inferior spirit, and withdrew.

Pluto had a well-drilled household. They never asked *why* such and such a thing was done—they immediately did it.

The Duke of Maldon was buried in the family vault in Dagenham Church, with the same "pomp and circumstance" which distinguished the obsequies of the late Sir Richard Fenacre. Messrs. Ghoul and Co., the eminent upholsterers of Saint James's Street, "undertook" the funeral; their talented foreman, Mr. Trestle, was in command, and everything was done in first-rate style. "William IV. didn't beat it," was Mr. Trestle's fiat in the housekeeper's room at Maldon Castle; " and as to that there Baronet we undertook at Fenacre, it was a mere 'one-horse' affair—almost work'us!"

Mr. Trestle did not really think so; he merely said it to flatter the Maldon domestics.

When we die, we may be quite sure that our servants will be keenly critical as to our funereal set-out. The autocrats of the kitchen will pronounce it "shabby," "mean," or "respectably decent;" and possibly, if Messrs. Ghoul undertake us, we may get a verdict of "a very pretty sight," or "a handsome affair," from those worthies. But of course, you and I, my dear readers, care nothing for the comments of John Thomas and Mary Anne, so we will pursue this dissertation no further.

Before leaving this grave subject, I must

relate an amusing little trait in Mr. Trestle's character. It is that worthy's habit to watch you and me, Mr. Methuselah, as we totter up the steps of our club in St. James's Street, or creep slowly into our brougham, with a very tender solicitude. He is nervously anxious as to our health, and when we do not drive up at our usual time, he will come to our area-gate, and ask our domestics how we are. John Thomas, to him.—"Master has gout flying about him. The doctor's been twice to-day, and ordered him water gruel, and knocked off his port."

"Ah! poor man," says the sympathizing Mr. Trestle; "he's not long for here." Then he goes back to Messrs. Ghoul, and says, "Old Methuselah will be a job for us before long; doctor's been twice. They'll have everything of the best!"

This last remark is purely professional,

and does not apply to your creature comforts in *this* life.

The next day he hears *I* am ill, and makes like tender inquiry.

However, you and I, Mr. Methuselah, do not mean to die yet: that is, if we can help it: and after a few days in bed, we are seen hobbling up the steps of the Fogies again.

Mr. Trestle sees us, and shakes his head ominously. "It's only a rally: the flare and flicker before the candle goes out," is his remark. *We* know better, however, and stir our stumps with the inciting truism, "There's life in the old dog yet;" and so we go on till the relentless reaper mows us down with that unsparing scythe of his, that pitiless sickle that spares neither youth nor beauty, but sweeps off alike the fair flower of the field and the ripened grain, the budding blossom and the withered rose! Down they all go before the sickle of that relentless reaper whose name is Death—down in a moment! In a moment all the bubbles of ambition are burst, all our schemes of aggrandizement laid in the dust, and we ourselves launched in that unseen, unknown, vast ocean of voidness, which lies beyond the confines of the grave.

Mr. Trestle had not so watched the Duke of Maldon because that nobleman died, as the *Times* said, suddenly, and at his place in Essex; but nevertheless he buried him with great pomp and splendour at Dagenham Church, and will be happy to do the same kind office by any of the readers of "Fenacre Grange."

Lord Henry was hastily summoned from Boulogne to attend his father's funeral. It was not without some feeling of fear that he landed at Folkestone: he looked upon every man he met as a possible bailiff, with a writ in his pocket to arrest him at the suit of Major Mandarin. However, his fears were not realized, and he walked with great solemnity at the head of the great black procession, in conjunction with his brother, the *ci-devant* Lord Dagenham.

This latter had now fulfilled the cause and purpose for which he had come into the world, or, in short, he had accomplished his mission: he had become Duke of Maldon!

And this, mark you, is no barren honour or mushroom peerage. The Fitzreines are *not* parvenus; their blood is of the bluest: it is azure in its tint! The Fitzreines came in with the Conqueror, and will probably go out with the " last man," whoever that desolate individual may be. They have a supreme contempt for the small fry of the Red Book, such as the law lords, and Nova

Scotian Baronets. In fact, they think nothing of a coronet that has not an Elizabethan origin, at the very least!

This being the case, our friend, if *we* dare to call him so, became a very great man indeed—almost a transcendant being to those who have not their names written in the book of Burke.

When the Duke's will was read, it was found that he had cut off his son Henry Fitzreine with a *shilling*, in consequence, it was stated, of his unfilial and unnatural behaviour about a certain *post obit*.

Now this was somewhat hasty of his Grace; but we know that he was a man of impulse, and seldom weighed any action, or lost time in putting a resolve into execution. He had altered his will, and signed it, and died. Therefore it became as unalterable as the laws of the Medes and Persians, which change not.

He died, like many "worldlings," very little lamented. His wife had known from the day of her marriage *what* her jointure was to be, and as it was a princely one, she was not inconsolable. Besides, a *dowager-*Duchess—I beg her pardon, the word is gone out of fashion—Maria, Duchess of Maldon, could still be one of the grandest of *grandes dames*, and a distinguished leader of the " best set" in society.

I think the plan of substituting the Christian name of a widow before her title, instead of that awful prefix of " dowager" scores 1 to the venerable body of *femmes passées*. If one wrote of the *Dowager*-Duchess of Maldon, you would all say "decided case of frump" at once; but as it is, you are not wholly disinclined to follow the fortunes of *Maria*, Duchess of Maldon. For all the public know, she may be young or even pretty (we who are behind the scenes know it is not so—but you, the benighted public, who read of her in the *Morning Post,* think she must be a transcendant being, blazing in diamonds). *We* know that she is an ordinary, disagreeable, not to say ill-tempered, middle-aged woman. If she had called herself " dowager" you would know it too, by instinct; but the Christian name as a prefix gives a charming ambiguity, and leaves room for the imagination to fill up details *au couleur de rose.*

A dowager conveys the idea of false fronts, false teeth, rouge-pots, violet powder, lapdogs, stays and padding, enamel and paint, and a general tone of artificial decoration — like a tumble-down old house covered with fresh stucco. A pretty Christian name may mean *anything.* Maria is *not* a pretty name; but then I did not give it to her Grace: it was the bad taste of her godfathers and godmothers in her baptism, not mine.

Well, to her ineffable horror, she found that her son Henry was absolutely dependent on her for *everything;* as he himself elegantly expressed it, " he hadn't one sixpence to rub against another." She could not let him starve, so she thought the cheapest way of supporting him was to take him to live with her at the jointure house in Grosvenor Square, where perhaps, after a short time, she might marry him to money.

"There are rich men in the east," said her Grace, " who would sell their souls to have a ' Lord' for a son-in-law, and I shall be able to manage it without much difficulty."

Maria, Duchess of Maldon, did not mean to procure a daughter-in-law from a Turkish harem, or a Rajah's palace in Hindostan, her thoughts merely wandered to the rich territory lying between Cheapside and Threadneedle Street. In that golden land the fathers like their daughters to marry "blood." "Hang it! sir," they say, "*I* find the money, and I expect some return for it: a certain percentage, a fair return. I could buy the whole beggarly lot of peers to-morrow, if I liked, but I'll have my girl marry 'blood,' sir!—there's nothing like it!" There's no toady like your free-born Briton, it is part and parcel of his very nature.

When her Grace was seated at breakfast one morning with Queen, a letter was brought in on a salver by one of the servants, addressed in a formal legal hand to "Lord Henry Fitzreine, 117, Grosvenor Square, W."

Queen changed colour as he read it: it was an application for the sum of two thousand pounds, owing by him to Major Mandarin.

"That fellow Mandarin again!" said he. "Confound him!"

"But you never signed the *post obit!*" replied the Duchess.

"No, but that doesn't do away with the fact of my owing him the money."

"How much is it, did you say?"

"Two thousand pounds," replied Queen, ruefully.

"Two thousand pounds!" exclaimed her Grace. "I suppose you expect *me* to pay it out of *my* miserable income, but I can't; that's a fact."

"I can't," said poor Queen, as he stared into the bottom of his tea-cup.

"You'd better go down and see Parchment about it. He'll find some way of getting out of it, if there is one," said his mother.

To this proposition Queen assented, and after breakfast sallied forth to the chambers of Mr. Parchment, which were situated in New Square, Lincoln's Inn.

Now Pluto, as we all know, is full of subtlety, deceit, and lies, and had sold the *post obit* the day after the Duke's death, before the will was known, to one of the children of Israel, for three-fourths of its nominal value.

He thereby secured a "lump" sum, and meant to sue Lord Henry for the whole amount of two thousand pounds which the *post obit* was meant to cover, hereby showing his craft and cunning. The Israelite who had bought the "paper" was a certain Michael Levy, famous in financial dealings with young men of good family and "expectations." Immediately after the Duke's funeral, Levy had taken steps to ascertain the contents of his will, and when he heard that Lord Henry was "cut off with a shilling," he, metaphorically speaking, lifted up his voice and wept, not for that poor young man's disappointment, but because it made the "*p. o.*" look, as he termed it, " deuced fishy."

Then he instructed his solicitor to take legal proceedings against Lord Henry Fitzreine.

When Queen got to Lincoln's Inn, he found the " enemy's" lawyer closeted with Mr. Parchment.

" This is a bad business, my Lord," quoth Mr. Parchment. " Very awkward business."

" *What's* an awkward business?" inquired Queen.

" The *post obit*, my Lord."

" The *post obit*," said Queen, with astonishment. " I never did one in my life! All some infernal mistake. Mandarin wanted me to, when I was in ' quod,' but I refused flat. I never *did* one in my life."

The two lawyers looked at one another incredulously.

"On the honour of a gentleman," continued Lord Henry, vehemently, "I never signed any *post obit* whatever."

"How much is it for, and who's it to?"

"For the amount of two thousand pounds, to the credit of Major Mandarin, transferred to that of Michael Levy," replied Parchment.

"It's a swindle," said Queen. "I do owe him that sum, but I never gave him a *post obit* for it; and to prove what I say, here is his application for the money I received this morning. As you will perceive, there is no mention made of any *post obit* in the letter."

"It's curious," said the lawyer. "What is the date of your borrowing the money?"

"I had it in three different sums," replied Queen. "The first on the 15th of March,

186—; and the second on May 7th, and the third, June 18th."

"What were the sums each time?"

"In the first instance, five hundred pounds; in the second, eight hundred and fifty; and in the third, six hundred and fifty."

"Let's see whether the dates and sum of money in the *post obit* coincide?" said Mr. Parchment. "Have you a draught of it with you?"

Mr. Dixon, the enemy's lawyer, had, and they examined it between them.

It set forth the following: that Henry Fitzreine agreed to pay Major Mandarin the sum of two thousand pounds at the decease of his father, the Duke of Maldon, in consideration of moneys lent him, respectively, on the 15th day of March, the 7th of May, and the 18th of June—viz., (1) 500*l.*, (2) 850*l.*, (3) 650*l.*—total 2000*l.*

"It's the same bill!" they all exclaimed.

"My client has been grossly imposed upon," said Mr. Dixon. "He's paid three-fourths of this sum in hard cash for a forged paper!"

Then they all agreed to make common cause against the common enemy, Pluto.

"I shall advise my client to indict him at once for a conspiracy to defraud," said Mr. Dixon, "and also for gaining money under false pretences."

"And I," said Mr. Parchment, "will watch the case on behalf of Lord Henry Fitzreine, whose signature he has forged."

In the course of the day, Major Mandarin was arrested at the suit of Michael Levy, for an attempt to defraud.

The case came on in a few days at the Old Bailey.

Mr. Small had been intrusted with the apprehension of Pluto, who shed brimstone tears at leaving his Hades. "It will go bad with me, I fear," was his remark. "I never did anything so awkwardly in my life."

His captor felt a grim satisfaction in his prey. "I have suspected him for years," he said, "but he's so cunning that I have never been able to be down upon him."

The Court was crowded when Baron Owl took his seat on the bench.

Everybody was quite quiet, but nevertheless the ushers shouted "Silence!" in stentorian voices.

Lord Henry was the first witness sworn, and after having kissed the book (oh! that greasy book), and murmured "S'help me," he was examined by the counsel for the defence.

"What is your name?" asked the bewigged barrister.

"Henry Fitzreine."

"Who gave you that name?" said a wag

in the crowd. A shout of laughter followed, which was instantly quelled by the ushers ejecting two old women who had never laughed in their lives, and who went cursing and swearing away at being balked of their morning's amusement.

"You signed a *post obit*, I believe?" said the counsel.

"No; that is, I was asked to, but I didn't wish, as I said at the time. I was asked to, but"——then he became confused.

"But *what*, sir?" said the counsel, in an awful manner; "but what, sir?"

"I don't know," said Queen, now hopelessly muddled.

"Oh! you don't know, don't you?" continued the counsel. "What *do* you know, because *I* should like to know it. You say you believe that you didn't sign a certain paper?"

"Yes."

"You said just know that you *didn't* sign the paper. Now you say you *believe* you didn't. There's a vast difference in that! Will you swear positively that you believe you signed the paper?" he continued rapidly.

"Yes," said poor Queen.

"Gentlemen of the jury, the witness now says he *did* sign the *post obit*. I think the prosecution will fall to the ground, gentlemen."

"Were you lodging at Mr. Moses's, in Whitecross Street, on the night of the 19th of June?"

"Yes."

"Did you cross to Boulogne on the night of the 19th of June?"

"Yes."

"Be careful, sir. You said just now that you lodged in Whitecross Street on the 19th, and now you say you crossed to Boulogne.

Be careful, sir!" Then he looked at poor Queen till he nearly sunk in his shoes.

"The fellow makes me out a liar before the whole Court. I swear I didn't mean to tell one," said Queen to himself.

Then Queen was told to stand down, and Mr. Michael Levy took his place in the witness-box. He stated plainly and positively that he had bought the "paper of Mandarin in the full belief of its genuineness, and had paid him three-fourths of the sum in cash, for which he showed receipts." Mr. Lynx, Pluto's counsel, could get nothing out of Michael Levy; so, after a few questions, he called for Henry Fitzreine again.

"Do you swear that your signature is a forgery?" said Mr. Lynx.

"I do, most solemnly," replied Queen.

Then Miss Moses was called, and, nothing

disconcerted, took her place in the witness-box, and gazed defiantly on the judge and jury.

"Do you remember Lord Henry Fitzreine sleeping at your father's house on the night of the 19th?"

"No," she replied; "he left at nine o'clock that evening."

"Will you swear he left at nine?"

"Yes."

"Mind what you are about; be quite certain before you speak. You'd better be careful. I ask you again, will you swear he did *not* leave the house at nine?"

"No."

"You said yes just now," said Mr. Lynx.

"That was because you put it another way. 'Yes,' is the answer to the *first* question; 'No,' to the second."

Mr. Lynx was, as he expressed it, "nonplused," and sat down, red in the face with rage, whilst a general titter ran through the Court, which was sternly quelled by the ushers.

Then Mr. Dixon rose and repeated what his client had stated, and at length came to the gist of the case, so to speak, namely, the forgery of Lord Henry's signature.

Queen swore positively he did *not* sign it, and Mandarin's only chance was to prove, by witnesses, that his statements were false. Miss Moses was his main reliance, the document purported to have been drawn up in the sponging-house, and her name was down as a witness. Miss Moses then swore positively that she had never witnessed this or any other signature; and after a few attempts on the part of Mr. Lynx to shake her evidence, the jury retired to consider the case.

In about half an hour they returned with a unanimous verdict—"Guilty."

Poor Pluto shook in the dock, and could only remain in a standing position by grasping the iron spikes.

The Judge then passed a sentence on him of ten years' penal servitude, prefacing with the usual formula of asking him whether he had anything to say in his defence.

"Only that Lord Henry and that girl are both liars. She let him out from the strong-room in Whitecross Street!"

"You're another," said Miss Moses.

"Remove the prisoner," said the Judge, sternly.

When Pluto felt the hands of the turnkeys on him, he fell on his knees and pleaded abjectly for mercy. He would do anything he could, only to be forgiven. But it was too late for mercy in the time of justice. They bore him out screaming. As soon as he got outside he became calm again, and with a careless laugh, remarked, "Checkmated at last!"

END OF VOL. II.

www.ingramcontent.com/pod-product-compliance
Lightning Source LLC
Chambersburg PA
CBHW032053230426
43672CB00009B/1581